HOME CLUTTER CLEANSE

AN ESSENTIAL STEP-BY-STEP GUIDE TO ORGANIZING YOUR HOUSE, OFFICE, AND LIFE BY GIVING ALL YOUR STUFF A *HOME*

ANNETTE MARIA WILLIAMS

HOME HARMONY

HOME
HARMONY

www.mediahomeharmony.com

CONTENTS

I am so thankful for my Lord and Savior Jesus Christ
and to my loving and supportive family!

INTRODUCTION

"If you fail to plan, you are planning to fail."

BENJAMIN FRANKLIN

I know the feeling! I was sitting on a bench at the beach this morning. I looked around and all I saw were two towels, two water bottles and four books. Only an iPad, and a magazine filled my bag—enough to keep me entertained for hours. But instead of relaxing with a good book, I found myself thinking about home and all the things I should be doing and all the projects I have left half done.

Day after day, you look around your house looking at piles of paper that you intend to organize someday. Closets stuffed with clothes that you know you will never wear. Kitchen drawers and cupboards with two of everything, an entranceway cluttered with shoes turned all in different ways. An old wrench, a screwdriver and unopened mail on the countertop mixed up with some of the groceries you didn't quite put away. Unfolded laundry still lay at the end of a couch and some new kitchen equipment that you bought on sale still unpacked on your countertop... and the list goes on and on.

About The Author

My name is Annette Maria Williams and I am a Professional Organizer. I enjoy organizing and working with people to become more organized themselves. I have worked with many clients and customers in their homes, businesses, and offices. I have learned that it is not about how much money you spend, but how you use what you have to get organized now! I have found that many people do not know where to start or think they are too disorganized to get organized. I have worked with clients with over 6,400-square foot homes to small one-bedroom apartments, so I know I can help you no matter what size home you reside in.

I think I was born to be a Professional Organizer. I didn't know for years that I was doing things that people would actually pay me for! I assumed that if I could do it, anybody else would do it just as well. I have since found that we all have different gifts and talents. Organizing a space gives me a sense of satisfaction, but the best part is seeing the relief on my client's faces at the end of the day.

It is so rewarding to help people achieve greater productivity and peace of mind. They feel less stressed and are at ease in their home or office, knowing that they can find their stuff! We have found items that people have been looking for for years, such as car titles, birth certificates, etc. Good organizers also set up systems that work for each of their clients to maintain. It is gratifying doing something that I enjoy and that comes easy to me and has wonderful benefits for others.

I'm a busy person. I've been pretty good about staying on top of my home in the past, but I have some old habits that can slowly creep back in. Writing this book has helped me stay focused and I want it to do the same for you. I have spent many years organizing homes and businesses, and I want to share my years of experience with you and give you the knowledge, tools, and support to get your home decluttered once and for all. I've taken all my experiences and created a system that has been proven effective with hundreds of people.

This book is not about giving you many solutions to figure out for yourself; it's about learning from my mistakes, other organizers, and my years of experience.

I am hoping you can get the most out of my suggestions and advice, so I placed as much material as possible into this book.

Professional Organizers

Professional Organizers often help people going through major life changes. Times of upheaval and stress such as a divorce, moving into a new home, death in the family, or possibly a new baby in the family can all be major stressors.

I know you are overwhelmed but still have great intentions of getting organized either on Saturday morning, some evening after work, or some other time soon. That time never seems to come because you're either too tired, or something more important always comes up. The clutter and disorganization in your home doesn't get better; it just gets worse. You know it affects you mentally because you are always tired and cannot relax because you have no place to relax.

Every room in the house is full of junk and clutter. You go out and leave it for a while, which is great, but guess what, you still have to come home to it. You may even experience some illogical thoughts like selling the house and moving because it would be easier, or the ultimate procrastination excuse: "If I can't do it right, I'm not going to do it at all."

You wish you could wave a magic wand to make it all go away, but in reality, you know you can't. Totally displeased with your situation, you would often find yourself muttering, "If I can get this place back in shape, I will never let this happen again."

Well, you're here...And that's a good thing.

You've obviously recognized that you have a problem and need some help. In all aspects of life, when the pain of the problem is greater than the pain of doing something about it, YOU CAN TAKE ACTION. The adage, "A cluttered home creates a cluttered mind, and in turn, a cluttered life," is absolutely true. It has been proven to lead to undue stress, anxiety, and physical problems like fatigue.

You're not alone.

According to the National Study of Organized Spaces (sponsored by Clutter, Inc.), a whopping 78% of North American households are disorganized and cluttered. A cluttered home doesn't have to be your reality. As a Professional Organizer, I work with people every day who have clutter and disorganization invading their homes. Still, through organization training and by following a simple formula, they can conquer their clutter problems once and for all.

I believe every person has the power to achieve a well coordinated home. If you're willing to dig deep and get proactive, and with some persistence, you too can have your home looking great in no time.

This book will guide you through every room in your home and show you how to organize with form, function, fashion, and a few humorous stories. I will also help give your home office a more professional look with an atmosphere enticing enough to work efficiently. My goal is for you to be organized and feel confident in your skills and abilities. I want you to know how to organize any space in your life: home, car, office, or garage. This book can help you unlock your natural organizational skills to make a better home for you and your family.

There may be a lot of eyesores in your house that are too much to handle. Instead of coming home to a blissful sanctuary, you often feel like you are marching into a war zone each time you enter. After a stressful day at work, you find your house giving you more stress than inner peace. Deep inside, you know you deserve better but you don't have a fair concept about the word organize. I am here to work that out with you.

I had been a Professional Organizer for many years when I first met Tina. She was a licensed pharmacist with two daughters, ages three and six. Her husband was in the Navy and was away for months at a time. I had trouble with my doctor's prescriptions one day and needed someone to rewrite what was written on that piece of paper for me, so I could understand the dosage schedule. She was so accommodating and helped me with other prescriptions. Because I was also a friendly neighbor, I invited her to my house for tea several times.

Each time she was there, I would notice her looking around, smiling. I would rather talk about some other things than ask how she found my house, so I just ignored it. Then, she started asking how I kept my house so clean and well-organized despite my busy job. Afterwards, I found out that her house was totally the opposite; she called it a jungle without the wild animals. For example, she brought home dozens of boxes of medicine samples and piles of unfinished paperwork that occupied most of her living room. Since she had been so helpful to me, I offered to help her too!

It pained her to let go of the boxes of medicine thinking she might need them in the future. With all the many boxes and piles of paper, random stuff, toys, and clothes, it filled all the corners of her house. With a lot of encouragement and assessment, I was able to convince her to donate the medicine samples to charity and sell belongings that were of less importance to her everyday routine.

With the help of friends, we sorted, purged, and organized her house inside out. With some tips and expert advice on organization and decluttering, she was amazed at the transformation. She now enjoys more space inside the home and was able to add a playroom and study room for her children.

Many events happen in life that we can't control, and at those times, people will need outside help. I have found that many people are shy about asking for help. I understand it can be uncomfortable if we are not organized or do not have our lives organized. It makes us feel like a failure! You are not a failure—it is brave and smart to recognize when we need help! I will address how and when to get help in my final chapter.

By the time you finish reading this book, I hope to have you transformed! You will be able to go into any room in your home or office and decide how to organize it. I will teach you how to declutter and make decisions about items you no longer need.

This is not just about organizing your home or your life. Getting organized will improve *every aspect of your life.*

I hope to help you make your spaces functional and beautiful. I can help you give all your items a logical "home." Efficiency = Less Stress = More energy to enjoy life!

You may think you don't have the time, but you can become organized with the following strategies.

If you have been keeping "stuff" in every corner, shelf, and closet of your home, you're not doing yourself any favors. If you've been thinking about getting more organized but aren't sure where to start, this book will help you out big time. Think of *S.T.U.F.F.* we all have to deal with: <u>S</u>pecial

Treasures and Unusual Fabulous Finds = S.T.U.F.F I have found that it takes more effort sometimes to keep stuff than to give it away.

We will go through each room together and decide what to keep, sell, donate, throw away, or recycle. We will create systems for you to use every day that will help you stay organized. You will be able to solve problems on your own and feel confident in your skills!

The goal is for you to declutter each weekend for several months until you have gone through your entire home.

You're not striving for perfection, as perfection in the realm of decluttering is a failure. You are likely a perfectionist, as perfectionism is a common trait of many who get disorganized.

You see, perfectionists generally will not undertake a project of any kind unless they can do it perfectly. However, the word *perfect* really does not exist in the perfectionist's mind, as nothing is ever *perfect* to them. Perfectionists, in reality, are *imperfect* people, like we all are, and perfectionism is linked strongly to anxiety.

To harness the power of perfectionism and get rid of all the clutter, you will need to stop striving for perfection and work within the normal perception of what is possible.

As you go through this book, I want you to have the strategies that can help you get the results you want in your life. I'm going to teach you how to implement a process that works.

Have you ever asked yourself why you are unable to change? You have probably experienced challenges on how to get your things in order and even struggled starting the process. Grab a hot cup of coffee, sit on a comfy couch and think.

Write down the three most important reasons why change is difficult.

What is stopping you from achieving your dreams and becoming who you want to be?

Now do some self assessment and decide what you are going to do about it.

There's nothing like being knowledgeable about home harmony. People around you may give advice but will only help a little, so this is where I come in.

The information you'll find in this book is powerful and effective. It has been the key to organizing hundreds of homes, businesses, and lives.

As you read along, you will develop your own style of decluttering, organizing and transforming your home so it can be an impressive living space for you and your family.

1

S. P. A. C. E

Creating space in your home means a lot of work. There are significant changes that need to be considered in every corner to make that space. It's important to remember that you can't change everything in a jif, you can work on it one step at a time. It's easy to get overwhelmed by the look of it, but giving up makes it worse. Start with the things you see every day, that's how you'll know where to begin.

I know it can be painful to get rid of an heirloom from your grandparents or the vase you got on your wedding day because of the attachment and old memories. But if you don't find the right place for them, they should go! Let's check out other pieces of memorable items that need to be stored properly to create more space.

Old stuff is also difficult to let go for the reason that you might need it in the near future. This is especially true if it was something you bought from your first salary ten years ago. It could be the patty maker in your cupboard that's been dusty for years and wasn't really useful nowadays, since patties are readily available in the supermarket. Why not put it in your "to sell" box? If you think of the money you can raise from selling old things you don't really use, that will be good motivation for you.

Check your seasonal inventory. You may have household essentials that should be changed every season. Seasonal items include winter clothes, footwear, and holiday decorations. To rid them out of places in the house they should not occupy, storing them in labeled boxes will do. Just work one zone at a time. Maybe start from the living room, which should be the most presentable. Take the labeled boxes with you to make sorting easier. That way, you'll know which box each item should go in. After packing everything neatly, you can store the boxes so they're out of sight until next year.

In this chapter, I will teach you to go through each space in your home and decide what to keep, sell, donate, pitch, or recycle. You can use this system every day in every room, and it will help you stay organized. You will be able to solve problems on your own and feel confident in your skills!

When you start decluttering and organizing, do this for every space in this order!

Mark 4 Boxes or Bags with the Following:

- Donate
- Sell
- Trash
- Belongs in another room

If it doesn't go into any of the above categories, then keep it in the room you are organizing.

Segregate things by taking them out of your closets, drawers, or cupboards in that space.

Almost all Professional Organizers use some form of the S.P.A.C.E. acronym to organize homes.

- **S-SORT**—items for that closet or entire room. Classify things according to use by putting all "like" items together! This will help you see what you currently own.
- **P-PURGE**—after sorting out the items, decide if you still need each item. If there are items you no longer use, donate them. Purge the duplicates. Do you really need eight wooden spoons? Part with things that you don't need so someone else can enjoy them!
- **A-ASSIGN**—a well-thought-out place for items you are going to keep. Don't just put it where it might fit; instead, put the item where it belongs and give it a "home!" Group *like* items together in a place that is convenient and logical. Kitchen utensils should go in the kitchen drawers and laundry detergents should be found in the laundry room. *Items need to be stored at the point of use!*
- **C-CONTAINERIZE**—Contain *like* items together. Do NOT go shopping for containers until after you have done the three

steps above! If you do, you will more than likely buy too many containers or containers that won't fit in the space. Containers can be boxes you already own. We do recommend clear containers the most because it is always nice to be able to see what is in the container. If you have ADD or ADHD tendencies, it is important to be able to find the items and put them away quickly. If you would like everything to match, you can purchase the correct size or different sizes of, for example, all white plastic bins or baskets. I prefer the plastic baskets since they are easier to keep clean. Use labels so you can remember, and each family member can learn where things "live." Label makers are worth their weight in gold!!

- **E-EVALUATE**—Now you need to make sure what you have done works for you and everyone in the household. Try it for a week, and if things aren't getting better, then get the family together to figure out why it is not working for everyone. Maybe you didn't leave enough room for the family's favorite breakfast items, or it's too high on the shelf for shorter family members, etc. Maintenance is an ongoing task, and you can always improve on what you started. Make sure it is in a logical home and make any adjustments needed to maximize function and aesthetics. Again, if you have ADD or ADHD tendencies, be flexible and don't be afraid to try something new.

For every room discussed in each chapter, the S.P.A.C.E. method will guide you through organizing that particular room. Remember, it is going to get worse before it gets better because you have to take everything out to sort and purge before you can do anything else!

The S.P.A.C.E. method will help you find a "home" for all the items you need to keep!

When we arrive at a consultation, we sit down with the client and ask them what rooms are a priority to them currently. Each consultation consists of listening to the needs of the client and creating a plan to reach the client's goals.

Cameras are a big part of our toolbox and help us do our job. Once we have discovered the rooms that need to be organized, we take photos of how it currently looks. We open up cabinets and drawers to get an idea of how they are storing things currently and the products they will need to declutter their space. After you have lived somewhere for a while, you often don't even see the things on the shelf or stuff in the corners. You can take photos of sentimental items, and if you think you don't need them any longer, we encourage you to donate the items. You can also use the photos for reference while shopping for bins and getting the right size and quantity. Then take photos again after reorganizing to see the difference. Some clients love seeing the before and after photos while they enjoy the improvements. I highly recommend you take before and after photos as we go through this process.

We also ask clients on the first work day if they are looking for anything. So many times we have found lost medical information, keepsakes and even the TV remote control!

But what is it like once you are through with your home?

Once your home is decluttered, it will feel completely different. You will be amazed at how much space you actually have! Every room will have an airy feel and will give you the freedom to redecorate.

TIP—Storing items at the point of use can save you so much time! I just had a client ask me where to store lunch bags/boxes. We told her to put them where the food is located, which would be the kitchen or pantry. Where do you keep cleaning supplies? Under the sinks in kitchens and bathrooms where they will likely be used.

2

LEARN THE MEANING OF FINDING A "HOME" FOR ALL YOUR ITEMS

"A place for everything, everything in its place."

BENJAMIN FRANKLIN

Home clutter is a growing problem for many people and it is so overwhelming. A home with too much junk in sight isn't relaxing at all. In urban homes, upgrading on a lot of things has become a trend, making outdated things pile up creating such enormous clutter, and before you know it, you've built a maze to your bedroom. Tying on new things isn't bad; we only need to be organized. There's a place for everything, and everything must go to its proper places.

In this chapter, you will learn the following:

Where do you most commonly store your items?

Whether you are a minimalist or a maximalist, decluttering will require the same organization and evaluation skills. The difference is in what you want to get rid of and what you want to keep. The principles that follow can be applied to either situation. We will find a home for all your stuff.

We will discuss the meaning of "living spaces" and what it means to have a tidy home, even if you have an overcrowded home.

Most people take pride in their "stuff." Having things you own is a sign of success or prosperity. But many people make more money than others yet still have less to show for it by how they live.

Let's get started!

Why is it easy to find your toothbrush every morning? If you are unable to find your toothbrush, that means there's something very wrong. Anyway, you can usually find your toothbrush every morning because you put it in the same place after each use. It has a home! The same should also be done with all the things in your house.

When my husband and I were first married, I noticed he was a little messy. I would find a lot of his stuff sprawled all over the living room floor while his garage was neat. He did not have the practice of putting things back where they belonged. I couldn't find the scissors because they were not in their "home." He kept wanting to find new "homes" for things and that never works! After talking it through, we agreed to bring things in order by labeling. Labels helped us find items easily and putting items back in their proper places after each use made life easier. We enjoyed our clutter free home and labels were also beneficial for the children as our family grew.

Organizing is creative problem-solving at its finest. You're always trying to figure out how to make something better. One of my classes in college was creating flowcharts. I loved it and have used that skill not only for information technology, but also to do paper flow analysis for different companies. Each job is a problem to solve.

I like to do things quickly and simply. I am a big believer in the K.I.S.S. theory: "Keep It Simple, Stupid." We often think that organizing makes things complicated when actually it's so simple. We are always trying to figure out how to make the most of every space with style and sustainability.

Handling your "to-do lists" and calendar is the first step in organizing. The busier you are, the more important a "to-do list" is. I once lost my mind working full-time. I had two young children with activities of their own, and a husband who traveled a lot and could not help me with the kids, or even pick up groceries. My mom was there to remind me of things to do because she knew I was having a rough time. I was so impressed she got things done while remembering my busy schedule. Then I realized she was retired at that time, so she didn't have a long list of things to do because she was not that busy. I tell young women today that, *yes, you can do it all, just not all at the same time!* There are seasons in life, for example, for working full-time, raising children, taking care of elderly parents, etc. We all need to figure out what is really important in life and if we are stressed to the max, try to slim down the list of activities.

Having a methodical "to-do" list that aligns with your goals will give you more control over the hours in your day. Consider using a timer initially as you start tackling chores to keep you on task. For example, set a timer for 30 minutes to get your calendar up to date. During that 30-minute timeframe, focus only on updating your calendar. Do not take phone calls, read text messages, or check emails, and avoid distraction in any way until the timer goes off. This helps you concentrate on one thing at a time, which will then help you focus on getting that one task completed. If you still need more time to finish the task after the timer goes off, take a quick break, reset the timer, and once again focus on the task until finished. You may need to do this while kids are napping or in school, so you won't be interrupted. Also, try and finish the items on the list that take the least amount of time first. That way, you will have fun checking off more tasks, and you have gotten more things done.

One way to be efficient with your time is to schedule different chores for different days. For example, do laundry on Mondays. That means to continue, you must be home. Since you are stuck at home for the day, this is a good time to pick up, dust, vacuum, and clean. Tuesday could be the day you get groceries, go to the post office, and do other errands. Try to schedule all this on one trip and map it out, so you are not backtracking and running all over town. If you work full-time, some of this may need to be moved to the weekend. Groceries could also be picked up on the way home. With so many stores now doing grocery pick-up, it's easy to go online, order your groceries, and schedule a pick-up time that works best for you. This also saves you time having to shop at the grocery store. It's great to pull up to the store and have a grocery attendant put your grocery bags right in the back of your car!

I know it's not always good for your brain to multitask, but thanks to modern conveniences, this can work—for example, start a load of laundry. While that's going, dust and vacuum the rooms close to the laundry room so you can continue to put clothes in the washer and dryer as the dusting and vacuuming continues. Unload the dishwasher before you start cooking a meal. Sometimes our dishwasher is used as an additional cabinet. Take out the clean plates, cups, and silverware that you will be using for that meal and put them on the table. Whenever possible, delegate to others. Children four and up can help set the table for dinner. As you cook, rinse the dirty utensils, bowls, etc., and put them right in the dishwasher. Once the meal is complete, have everyone bring their dishes to the kitchen sink, rinse, and put their dishes in the dishwasher. Start the load of dishes, and then relax or go for a walk!

Brain Drain

I encourage my clients to do a daily "brain drain" to get all those "to-do lists" out of their heads into a notepad. This helps get the clutter out of your mind. I also put the free ColorNote App on my phone when I am on the go. When I think of something I need to be reminded of later, I open the app and type a quick note. After which is transferred to my calendar or grocery list, or delete the completed task entirely. This has really helped me remember the things I need to get done. Scheduling appointments on your calendar helps a lot.

There is a big difference between "scheduling" something on your calendar and just "planning" to finish that task. It makes you feel refreshed to cross out items off your brain drain list when completed, knowing that you are making progress. It is also important to keep your priorities in mind, like business meetings and phone calls, laundry, meal planning, time for family and friends, etc. Write these things down in the front of your notepad and check them frequently to help you stay focused on your priorities. If the "to do" list does not align with your priorities, then rethink what really needs to be done and prioritize accordingly. Before saying "yes" to something new, take a moment to pause and ask yourself if that commitment aligns with your goals. Our days are limited to 24 hours; when you say "yes" to one thing, you are saying "no" to something else. Spread out chores to others if possible to lessen your daily workload. This buys you time for personal activities you've missed doing. Maybe you'd like a strawberry sundae topped with lots of cream and chocolate sprinkles at a nearby park to relieve you from stress. Maybe you would like to fuel up at the coffee shop next to your block. By the time you're back home, you'll be more than ready for another decluttering battle.

Also, schedule time on your calendar weekly to maintain the well-organized systems you create—find time to pick up clutter, tidy living spaces, file papers, meal plan and prep, stay current on the kids' schedules, etc. It only takes 30 days to create a habit (good or bad), and it becomes a way of life.

Make your calendar simple and manageable. It should only take one click to remind you of certain appointments and make each hour run smoothly. Don't keep adding any other activities on your blocked time. To keep you on track, make sure to wrap up what you have started in your first schedule before starting another. If something doesn't get done on the day it is scheduled, then reschedule it at the next available time on your calendar. Group like activities together for efficiency. Consider using different colors on your calendar to distinguish visually what appointments involve you versus family members.

When you start the organizing process on your own, do it slowly to make the process less overwhelming. Rushing is stressful and draining. Check on your availability and other schedules to know when to get started. It's easier to find decluttering solutions when there are no other things nagging at you.

Clean as you go; don't let messes build up in the first place. If you are in motion and see something that isn't right, bring it with you. Bring a glass of water into the living room, take it back to the kitchen when you get up. Make washing dishes or loading the dishwasher a part of the process at the end of the meal time. Chairs are not coat racks, counters are not shelves, and floors are not wastebaskets. Gather up elements that don't belong to keep the room fresh.

We call "prime real estate" the areas that are shoulder height to knee height. Put items in these areas that are used often. Of course, that can be different for different people. I am short, so the top shelf in my kitchen is for storing things I only use once a year or for special occasions. Some people have issues with their knees or back. Items used more often must be put where you can get to them easily; for example, if you have back issues and can't bend very far, don't place them on the bottom shelf.

Place items into appropriate, clear containers—more on this later depending on the room.

Keep ONLY items you love and use frequently!

Decluttering and organizing take a lot of time and hard work. So don't beat yourself up while you're learning. Keep your focus on your goal, not on where you have been.

Start with one room or closet at a time. For example, for the next six Saturdays, take one closet each week and be sure to use the S.P.A.C.E method in Chapter 1. If you take it slower you will also get used to the places you've stored your things.

If you are already overwhelmed, start with the smallest closet first. When you see how nice it looks and how much more room you have, you can go on to bigger areas—perhaps the laundry room.

The benefits of being organized are many. It can save you money because you won't buy a certain item again that you are unable to find. It saves you time because you have an assigned place for your items, and you can get to them quickly!

Before I get started, I want to share with you a story that demonstrates the power of organizing and what you can accomplish with it.

Just after high school, my cousin got married to a great guy and had her first part-time job. But she had an awful pregnancy with hard complications, so her husband left his work for a while to look after her. Good thing—she delivered a healthy baby boy. Now, with all the significant changes that motherhood entailed, she had a difficult time organizing the house they'd just moved into.

One day, I went to help my cousin organize her new bedroom set. The job went smoothly because all the materials we needed were neatly kept in the garage. She said she was happy to have stored her stuff that way for future use, since she wasn't really sure exactly when she could redo her bedroom set again. Whether she would decide to put her bedroom set back together in the next ten years or earlier, it would be easy for her to find the boxes and materials.

We tend to write down things we want to complete every day, only to find out later that they are not important. We sometimes get confused with our priorities and making "to-do" lists won't work. This is where the power of organizing comes in. Designing a specific storage in your house where you could easily reach items you constantly use and making it a habit to return things in their proper places works best.

The things that have been added to our lives that we want to keep don't really count as clutter. The stuff that still has value and use, but needs to go, will cause us the most stress.

Every time you open a box or take out an item, and it doesn't upset you, then you are getting closer to your goal of saving some valuable space!

You need to know where all your things are in order to keep them organized. What's happening is that we are leaving it up to chance or the randomness of organizing. We're not living in control anymore—and we don't have a system that works for us.

Key Takeaways from This Chapter

1. Consider the visual effect it has on you when you see a cluttered area and figure out how it can remind you of your entire life.
2. Start with small areas—closets, etc. and work on one room or one closet at a time—perhaps a bedroom per week or one day a month.
3. Keep all your appointments on one calendar; schedule appointments with yourself and keep them as if you were in a business meeting.
4. Always keep your system simple and focused on your vision for yourself—don't try to be perfect, just get it done!
5. Create a system where you can always find and access your items with ease.

6. Have an action plan that allows you to remain flexible and able to change quickly if necessary; remember to do a daily "brain drain."

The next chapter discusses both small and large spaces. I will explain the best way to organize your items in spaces like entryways, command centers, drop zones, laundry rooms, and mud rooms. We will discuss ideas for each of these areas.

3

ENTRYWAYS, COMMAND CENTERS, DROP ZONES, LAUNDRY ROOMS, AND MUD ROOMS

"Work at getting organized is like a hobby. Set aside a certain amount of time each day (or whatever time your budget will allow). While it may indeed take a fair amount of time to establish order, once it is achieved, you will save more time than you have ever spent."

DENIECE SCHOFIELD

Have you ever looked at the door of your home and felt overwhelmed?

We all have too much stuff and too little space for it in our homes. And the doorway is always a central point that tends to look chaotic.

But then, using just a few simple steps, you can sweep the mess away and revel in your organized space!

This chapter will teach you how to declutter your entryway or other areas near the front door. We'll also discuss command centers and drop zones, so you can keep your home more organized.

This chapter will cover the following points:

The difference between entryways, command centers, drop zones, and mud rooms.

We'll start with a discussion about what an entryway is and why it's important to keep it organized.

You'll also learn some basic organization methods for keeping entryways, mud rooms and command centers organized, as well as how to simplify your life through using these areas efficiently for everyday tasks.

Although there are a number of ways to organize a home, we have found that creating an entryway area that's easy to get into and provides a fun and visual display is key to keeping your entryway organized.

You'll also learn about the power of command centers and how you can use drop zones as a way to get everything into your command centers.

We'll look at the difference between clear, open, and closed storage space and how to arrange both storage and décor items in a way that helps you keep things neat and tidy while still allowing some leeway to create your own form of organization.

It's important to note that despite the many ideas you can adapt for your home and situation, don't feel bound by them. They are merely suggestions. You can decorate your command centers to fit with your tastes and needs; after all, it is your home! And you don't want to feel like you have to do things a certain way to fit in with anyone else's ideas.

Don't worry, we will discuss why we did this in each step and how you can personalize the command centers in your home.

Let's start with our first step.

Entryway

The entryway should be the cleanest area in the house because it gives your guests the best impression of you. Imagine a guest who might be hesitant in entering because of a cluttered entryway. To give it a welcoming feel, it should always look tidy and organized. To do that, here are some things you should do and remember.

Seeing all sorts of stuff scattered on the floor and unsightly, forgotten things behind the door can make you cringe. You want your entryway to be an area that helps you feel calm and ready to tackle whatever is coming at you from the outside world.

A clean, crisp and fresh entryway is as important as wearing your most charming smile because it is the gateway to your castle. But again, getting it organized and inviting can be overwhelming.

Let's take a look at the components of an organized entryway.

Rugs

Rugs are not only decorative, they also add comfort and warmth to your home. Rugs help keep your home clean too! Place an outside mat/rug at the entrance to all the doors that enter your home. Then you can put a nice rug on the floor in the doorway into your home. With both rugs, you should be able to keep most of the dirt from the outside coming in. If you are like my family, it's even better to take your shoes off at the door to keep your floors and carpets clean.

Rugs can come in many different colors and designs. If you want a simple, yet large one, a rectangular or oval suits well. Color, prints and fiber types are also elements to consider. You may want to choose something that matches your decorations.

Sometimes we would choose durability over style. Rugs come in different fibers and textures. If you want durability and style in one, there are wool rugs that have modern designs to suit your design preferences and last longer. Wool rugs are perfect for entryways and living room areas because they can withstand dirt and are easy to clean.

Let's take a look at another area that is often overlooked when it comes to organizing an entryway: The décor.

Décor

Décors are another important element in your entryway. The décor of your entryway is the first thing that people see when they come into your home. It can make or break their first impression when they walk in, and it's something people tend to look at before making a decision on whether or not they want to stay.

For a pretty and inviting effect, we recommend hanging multi-purpose pieces on walls to serve as decorations and storage at the same time. Catch-alls with decorative pockets or hooks are amazing accents and make the area more organized. The pockets can catch car keys, coins, phones, notepads and pens or anything you've kept in your pockets.

A decorative large basket can also serve as an umbrella rack or just something to liven up a boring doorway. These baskets can be accented with a hat or scarf or a bunch of dried flowers to complete the ensemble. Also make sure that other decorations in the entryway are dual purpose to keep the area clutter free.

When it comes to décor and organization, we recommend having your décor reflect the style of the home or room that you want people to walk into when they enter your home. If you want to create the vibe of a country farmhouse, then we recommend having your décor reflect this. There are baskets out there that are perfect for providing visual interest. The old baskets and pails actually make very nice units when it comes to décor, as long as you make sure there is enough space to fit the items you're putting in them.

One type of décor that will never go out of style is plants. As long as you take proper care of them, plants will always be great for adding color and décor to the home. Plus, you can move them around from room to room or from entryway to entryway in order to help with transitioning throughout the house.

If you want more décor for your entryway, we recommend shopping at stores such as Hobby Lobby, Michael's or Joann's. They have everything from baskets to flowers, and the prices are affordable. If you do go this route, here is a tip to help make your trip less expensive: get a coupon for the store before shopping there. You can usually find coupons online or in newspaper ads.

Try picking pieces that go together in style and shades to create character in your entryway. There will always be something perfect for the door itself. A lot of us love hanging eye catching door decors especially during the holiday season.

Aside from dried flowers, live plants in artistic pots and vases add charm to an entryway. There are ornamental plants with beautiful leaves that are perfect when indoors. To create a more inviting aura, fresh flowers can have a place on your console table.

You can decorate anywhere from the front door to the living room area in your entryway. Mirrors are wonderful at making a small space feel larger.

If you are looking for some last-minute decorating ideas, then we recommend checking in with your local home or craft store. They often carry seasonal décor or even have DIY kits that will allow you to create some decorative pieces. Another place for great decorating ideas is Pinterest.com

Benches

Benches are a nice addition to any entryway. They are a place for you to sit so you can catch your breath and relax for a moment. Benches are a great place to take off or put on shoes too. The bench is even better if it allows a place to store shoes underneath for easy access.

If you are going to purchase a bench for your entryway, then make sure it's sturdy enough. It can be a great place for your guests to put down their purse or perhaps return an item they borrowed from you. Make sure the bench colors are attractive and the painting job is done well so it adds beauty to the entryway.

Hooks

If there is room above your bench for hooks on the wall, this makes a great place to hang coats and hats. Make sure and invest in durable hooks and attach them to the wall securely so they will hold heavy coats.

Hooks involve much less work than hangers. They are easier for children. Place them low enough so your children can hang up their own coats, backpacks, and gear.

Hooks are also very useful for keys. Keys can be placed on a hook underneath a box hung on the wall for incoming or outgoing mail. If you purchase a key hook, then you'll need to make sure it's placed where it's easy for people to reach. This is important because if it is too hard for someone to reach the key, then they will probably be less likely to hang it up when they enter your home.

Bins

The bench and bins or baskets can set a threshold on what it can hold. The bins/baskets can hold essential items (shoes, caps, gloves, etc.) while hiding the clutter. Jackets and shoes that are actually being worn go here. Think of this piece of furniture as your "grab and go" items—NOT storage.

When you hang items on hooks, the hanging part is usually low enough to get under. Decorative bins are great if you have little ones or if you are trying to keep things accessible for children. It also allows you to have them closer to the floor where it's easier for children to reach. You will likely need a step stool for your kids to get items from the upper bins, but that's ok because they can easily place their items in and then put the bin up once they're finished.

You can also use stackable drawers. The drawers allow for easy access when stacked two or three high. This is nice because you want to create quick and easy storage solutions.

Mud Room and Coat Closet

The coat closet holds the jackets, shoes, winter wear, etc. so the entryway bench or hooks won't be overwhelmed with too much "stuff." Empty the hooks or hall tree weekly and put the coats and hats in the coat closet. A door-hanging shoe organizer (with clear pockets) can be mounted on the inside of the closet door. This is a great place not only for shoes but also for hats, gloves, caps, scarves, etc.

Vertical space inside closets is almost always overlooked. Over-the-door storage options utilize vertical door space as storage for a variety of items. The clear shoe organizers can also hold craft supplies, cleaning supplies, toiletries, small toys, etc. Consider this type of storage on any door in your home (bedroom, bathroom, laundry room, closets, etc.) to maximize storage using your vertical door space.

I have a behind-the-door cabinet that I just love! It is a narrow, tall cabinet that attaches to the back of a door. It is easy to install as it goes on the hinges of the existing door and can hold wrapping paper, medicine, craft or office items, etc. It has a magnetic closure, so it can even go on the back of a guest bedroom door and look nice. This is great for apartments or rentals because it can easily be taken off the hinges and moved to your new place.

Many homes have a flight of stairs close to the entryway. If yours does too, you can put a cute basket at the bottom of the stairs to gather toys, clothes, papers, etc. that need to be returned to their proper homes upstairs. This keeps you from running up and down several times a day to put just one item away. Buy a matching basket to keep at the top of the stairs for the same reason.

For the shelf in the closet or mudroom we recommend the Sterilite storage boxes for a variety of reasons. First, they come in different sizes such as 12 x 12 inches and 6 x 18 inches, and you can find them at any number of stores including Target, Wal-Mart, or online at Amazon. They are also stackable, for small spaces. Plus, they are usually made out of a strong plastic material. They will be able to take the weight you put on them without bending too much, even if you have a lot of heavy items stored in them.

We recommend using baskets for smaller items as we discussed previously and plastic totes for larger items that are easily seen and can be pulled down from a high place. There are lots of storage containers but always try to get clear ones so it is easy to see what is in them. If you don't like the look of clear containers then be sure and get some pretty labels to label what is in each bin. It is easy to forget where you put things when you first start organizing so labels are very important!

Drop Zone or Command Center

Some people call these "launching zones" since they are where the family *rockets* out the door or where everything lands when coming home.

Many kitchens have built-in desk space, which make great home command centers. The top drawer is a great space for pens, pencils, paper, binder clips, paper clips, etc. Expandable dividers work in most drawer spaces.

Each week, you may have mail or kid's papers that have to be signed and returned, bills to be paid, etc. Have a spot set up in your command center so these papers can be dropped in one designated spot. Think of it as a to-do box. We will talk later in more detail about children's papers.

If you don't have a kitchen desk, a spot on the countertop close to an outlet could house your phone for your charging station. If counter space is very limited then I recommend a socket shelf that goes over a wall outlet that can hold your phone. They even have these with additional outlet ports. A small shallow drawer organizer in the top drawer close to this area would be great for organizing office items like pens, staples, paper clips, rubber bands, etc. Another drawer could be used to hold your calendar, reminder notebook, and grocery list. Papers don't have to be filed immediately if you have a box to hold the bills and label them "to be filed" or paid. Another file would be "action file." Be sure and check this daily or put notes on your calendar.

So many of our clients have daily Amazon deliveries. Open the box, put the box in the recycle bin, then put the items away. If you let boxes stack up in the entryway, kitchen, and living room, it gets overwhelming to deal with. If you deal with it upon arrival, it makes the job much easier, and you can control the clutter.

If you don't have time to put things away immediately—say after dinner—go through the items just brought home. Clean out the lunchbox and make lunch for the next day. Once homework time is over, get the backpack and put it back on the bench or hook for quick access while you head out the next morning. Planning for the next day is very important! It will help you get out the door and to your appointments on time. Items needed before you go out the door (things to return to a store, shopping lists, packages to mail, etc.) should be put in one spot close to the exit the night before so you can grab and go! Call it the "To-Go" box!

Laundry Room

Don't forget, if you lose a sock in the dryer, it comes back as a plastic lid that doesn't fit any of your containers!

Rules of the laundry room—sometimes this is the catch-all room. Since laundry rooms can just be hall closets or big enough to have large craft rooms, I will give you a general idea of what to store in this space. If you have a laundry room that is large enough for a side-by-side washer and dryer and storage cabinets or shelves on the wall, then this is what I suggest.

Keep all laundry products and laundry baskets handy while doing your laundry. If you have a small laundry room, they do make collapsible laundry baskets that can be stored by hanging on the wall. The wall mount ironing board cabinet that fits in the wall between the studs that pulls down when needed is very handy for small laundry rooms. too It folds up, and there will still be enough room to store the iron and any spray products needed inside the cabinet.

Laundry room cabinet storage is great not only for laundry supplies, but also for cleaning products, utility storage, extra light bulbs, extension cords, and a small toolset for quick fixes around the home. You should have a rod for hanging items to dry. If it is close to the kitchen, you can store extra paper products such as paper towels, paper plates, and napkins. You can also store picnic items such as tablecloths and plastic ware.

If you have enough wall space, a wall-mounted mop/broom holder is very handy to hold lots of cleaning items. Small vacuums can also be hung on hooks on the wall.

A folding drying rack is a nice addition to any laundry room. They don't take up much space and are easy to mount.

If you have shelf space in your laundry room, I highly recommend a wire shelf instead of wood. They don't collect as much dust, and it is easier to see items on the shelf. They are simple to mount, and you can also hang clothes on hangers on the edge of the wire shelf for temporary drying or organizing.

Clear plastic shoe boxes you get from the store, such as Wal-Mart or your local dollar stores are great in the laundry room for holding products such as light bulbs, tape, cleaning rags, etc. You can use these shoe boxes throughout your entire home, not just in the laundry room.

Every laundry room needs a small garbage can (and extra liners) for dryer lint and other trash. Storing batteries in the laundry room is a good idea. Studies have found that heat can damage batteries. Putting them in the refrigerator can extend their life, so we keep ours in our garage fridge. If you don't have room in your fridge for your batteries, then the next best place is the laundry room.

If your laundry room has a limited footprint, it should NOT be used as a "holding spot" for laundry (dirty or clean). Schedule specific laundry days on your calendar. During laundry day, you would wash, dry, fold, and put away all your laundry. Dirty clothes remain in dirty clothes hampers in their respective bedrooms until laundry day arrives. You may need two or three laundry days scheduled on the calendar each week to stay caught up. If you have children, teach them to bring their dirty clothes to the laundry room. They can learn to sort clean socks and put away their own clothes. Children need to be involved so they can learn to do their own laundry when they get older.

If you have pets, and the laundry room is big enough, this is also a good space to keep their pet supplies, food, and water bowls.

Cleansing clutter in entryways, command centers, drop zones, laundry rooms, and mud rooms will create an easy to manage, stress free life for you. Proper organization is key to a peaceful home!

My friend Kathy had been married for about four years after meeting her husband at work. Their home was messy and disorganized, and she had a hard time finding things. The entryways were always piled high with magazines, kids' toys, mail, coats, and shoes. Getting tired of seeing the clutter build up around the doors of her home, she thought it was time for a change.

Kathy had decided to start a new tradition to help her family in keeping the entryways clutter-free. She picked a specific day of the week and put it on their family calendar. That particular day became Entryway Day. Every Saturday, they focused on putting all the clutter from around the doors back into their rooms and closets, and then wiping down and refreshing whatever was there. Then, when they were done, she would take pictures of what it looked like before they started (and after).

The next week, she took pictures of the entryway, and then put all the things back into their respective rooms. She wrote a note that said "Entryway Cleanup" (or whatever they decided to name the new day). She shared these pictures with her family and enjoyed seeing their reactions to their entryway being clean and organized.

This brought joy to their home and peace to their entryway because she was teaching her family that cleanup must be every single day's responsibility. If we don't make a priority to keep our home tidy, then it will be filled with chaos and clutter, and our lives will become incredibly stressful as a result. We are stewards of our home, so let's make sure it is in good shape for everyone to enjoy!

Fun tip—if you have a large family, and sorting socks has become a big issue, you can try this. Since most of us have white socks, color-coordinate them for each member of the family. For example, my husband's white socks always have gray toes and heels, my white socks always have pink or purple toes and heels. Kids' socks can be done the same way with whatever color is their favorite. Color coordinating socks can make sorting much faster. If you have too many of the same color currently, another idea is when the socks are dirty, have a hanging mesh bag in their closet, and that would be where the dirty socks go. At laundry time, just throw the mesh bag full of socks in the washer and dryer, and then all their socks would stay together to be returned to their bedroom dressers. Once their socks are put in the dresser, hang the empty mesh bag back in their closet to continue to contain the dirty socks. If you don't get laundry done in one day, you could buy two mesh bags so you always have one in the closet.

Key Takeaways from This Chapter

This chapter covered decluttering the entryways, command centers, drop zones, laundry rooms and mud rooms. The key takeaways are:

- **Entryways**—make sure your entryway is inviting to your guests. Keep it organized and don't let it become clutter central. Having clutter there does not make a good first impression and it's not comfortable for anyone.
- **Mud Room and Coat Closet**—every season go through the coats, hats and gloves to be sure they fit and are still in good shape. Donate the items that no longer fit.
- **Command Centers and Drop Zones**—make sure these are organized, and if they do get cluttered, clean up the clutter as soon as possible.
- **Laundry Rooms**—great place to keep not only laundry supplies but overstock such as paper products and party items.

The next chapter will cover how to organize your kitchens and pantries.

4

HEART OF THE HOME - KITCHENS AND PANTRIES

"[...] *The kitchen is a place of adventure and entirely fun, not drudgery. I can't think of anything better to do with family and friends than to be together to create something.*"

TED ALLEN

The kitchen can be the worst. It can make anyone feel like throwing in the towel when it comes to decluttering. But once you've implemented S.P.A.C.E—refer to Chapter 1 for details—and your little habits to keep it tidy, you'll want to celebrate how far you've come. You'll be able to spend time in your kitchen without staring at all the clutter.

If your home is designed well, the distance from your car/garage to your kitchen should be short. In other words, the garage door or entrance to the house should only be steps from the kitchen. What do we carry in the most from the car? Groceries! Get in the habit every time you enter your home with groceries or purchases in hand to put them away where they belong, immediately! The few minutes spent doing this minimizes the clutter that will collect in corners, counters, and floors.

Everyone can cook! Some enjoy it more than others. This chapter will help make cooking faster and easier.

Cooking is NOT one of my favorite things to do, so I try to keep it as simple as possible. My favorite cookbooks are meals in 30 minutes or less, and I love my crockpot. I would be at work and think, I am cooking, and when I get home, it will be ready. Crockpots can save you when you have a busy schedule, and many members of the family will be eating at different times. It can get especially crazy if you have several children that are all doing sports.

Kitchen Cabinets and Drawers

To declutter your kitchen cabinets and drawers, empty out everything on your counters or table. Sort likes with like. Purge everything you will not use or eat, meaning donate unexpired food to a local food bank and discard anything that has expired or is no longer consumable. Less is more, and we can all take out kitchen utensils we're not using and only keep those that will fit in the drawer. Do you really need three identical soup ladles? If not, donate some so someone else can use them. Wipe and clean the cabinets and drawers thoroughly once they are empty. If you have a large kitchen, see if you can get a friend or relative to help. It keeps you on task and can be fun to have a helper. Tell them you will return the favor at their house.

Shelf Liner—If you happen to be just moving into your home, I suggest putting in shelf liners in the kitchen before move-in day if possible. This is a big project, and I would suggest just doing a few cabinets at a time since, again, you will need to take everything out of the cabinet. Each shelf and drawer should be wiped down before the shelf liner is put in place. The process is not at all challenging, but it is time-consuming. I recommend a clear rigid liner that is easy to work with but still adds cushion and spill protection. These come in 12" widths and are good for upper shelves and pantries. Then, there is a wider width that is good for lower cabinets and under sinks. I would NOT recommend adhesive liners, as the glue in some brands attracts bugs, and these liners can be difficult to remove. Others have holes in them that allow spills to go right through them. There are many options at the marketplace—find one that fits your style.

If you happen to have a Lazy Susan Cabinet in the corner of your kitchen, there are clear corner containers that work great in these areas.

Coffee/Tea Breakfast Center

I am not a morning person. I want very few lights on and don't want anyone to talk to me until I have had my tea or coffee in the morning. Until that point, it's just not pretty. With that being said, I really like what I call a simple breakfast center. I can get the tea or coffee started quickly and my other food going, and I try to wake up. I would suggest a beverage and breakfast zone. Creating an actual beverage area in your kitchen area will allow you to maintain the counter areas.

Frequently used coffee and tea items should be near the coffee maker, making it simple to put things back after being used. The toaster and any vitamins or protein powders can be housed in the beverage zone. Anything you would use in the morning should live in this area; oatmeal, bagels, cereal, sugar, etc. are here for convenience.

Your kitchen should provide quick and convenient access to items you use every day. A kitchen functions most efficiently when divided into zones that best fit your needs: a food prep zone with clear counter space; a cooking zone near the stovetop with your spices, pots, pans, and stirring utensils nearby; glasses near the sink or fridge; dishes near the dishwasher and/or table, etc. The cabinets and drawers within easy reach are "primary real estate." Keep things you use often in your primary real estate zones. Lesser used items can live in the uppermost cabinets. For example, fine china overstock can be stored in protective storage cases in the upper cabinets. The cabinet above the refrigerator could house oversized party items that are used only for large gatherings.

Once you zone the kitchen, label the inside edge of a drawer or cabinet door so it's obvious what should be stored there for everyone who lives in the home.

Some large kitchen tools can get jammed in the drawers and won't stay put. Instead of crowding drawers, move the large ones (for example, the accessories to your countertop mixer) to the insides of the cabinet door. Place small 3M Command Hooks above or below the shelf level so they don't block the door and hang tools on the inside of the doors.

There are several ways to store spices: drawer liners, turntables, or drawers that fit in the cabinet. Whatever style you use, be sure and store spices in alphabetical order, so you can find them quickly.

Get some inexpensive shelf inserts from your local dollar store or Wal-Mart if you need more cabinet storage space. This can double the size of your storage and make things easier to get to because items are not stacked on top of each other! Wire shelves can be useful in adding shelf space throughout your kitchen. These shelves come in various sizes, and some expand to fit the space. A divider that allows vertical storage for platters, pans, baking sheets, lids, and cutting boards allows easy access to items that are often stacked. Several drawer dividers are helpful to organize kitchen utensils and gadgets. We recommend that oils and spices be stored in cabinets next to your stovetop. Turntables are good for oils and tall items. One spin of the turntable brings what you want to the front of the cabinet, and spills will be easily caught by the turntable. Be sure and measure each cabinet before buying a product because each cabinet in the kitchen can be a different size.

A kitchen is a high-priority space, since everyone in the household uses it. Schedule a time on your calendar to work on meal planning, grocery shopping, and meal prep for the week. When possible, prep food items ahead of time. While cooking, put things away as you go to keep things tidy. For example, if you're done with the milk, put it back in the fridge. If you're done with a spice, return it to its home, etc.

Determine when you need meals to be ready and work backward, time-wise. If you start with an empty dishwasher, you can tidy up while cooking. Wash or put items in the sink or dishwasher as you go.

Expired food! We had one client that loved buying in bulk. They thought they were saving money. They probably did with non-perishable items like paper towels and toilet paper (they were soo prepared for Covid because they literally had a linen closet full of toilet paper). The problem was the food. We threw away probably six large trash bags of food that had expired. There were only three members in the family—parents and one child, so they couldn't eat it fast enough to justify buying in bulk. It's not always cheaper, and if you don't have space, just buy what you need when you need it. Usually, two weeks' worth of paper products, food, and water will get you through most storms or panic buying.

Recipes—We all have our favorites. They can be from grandma or something you found on the back of a box, from a cookbook or magazine, or online. Keep the paper monster at bay by putting everything you can on your computer. Either scan the recipe or type it into a word document. So many of us have shelves of cookbooks we never open. Go through each book, pick out your favorites, scan them, and then donate the book. You will be much more likely to use the recipe because it will be much easier to find. I like to keep my recipes in order by main ingredient under the recipes folder on my laptop. The title of the document in the recipe folder is, for example, if I have chicken, I go through my chicken recipe documents: Chicken Chili, Chicken Pecan, etc. Then, I open the document to see if I have the other ingredients to make the dish.

Be efficient with your time. For example, buy several pounds of ground beef when it is on sale, cook it all at one time, and then make several meals out of it: hamburgers, sloppy joes, tacos, soup, casseroles, etc. Double recipes and freeze half for the days you don't have time to prepare meals from scratch. Same idea when chicken goes on sale. Cook it in bulk and have roasted chicken one night, then chicken pot pie, chicken salad, enchiladas, etc. This simplifies meal prep time and gives you a backup plan (frozen meal prepared two weeks ago) on really hectic days. Consider a weekly rotation of favorite meals so each family member has a favorite meal each week. This helps everyone appreciate the time and effort you are putting into this very important task.

To help with grocery shopping, check your produce drawers and toss out the unusable item in the drawers. Since most refrigerators have two produce drawers, move the good product to the left drawer. When you buy new products, put them in the right drawer. You can label the inside of the drawers so everyone in the family will know what needs to be consumed first.

Glass storage containers are best for leftover food. You can see what is inside; they freeze well and can be warmed up in the microwave.

Food storage containers are often a challenge for those who actually love to cook and have leftovers that need a home. There are two food storage products in the market that provide great storage options while requiring a small storage footprint. Rubbermaid sets provide a wealth of sizes while minimizing one's footprint due to their nesting capabilities.

The best place for pickles, olives, dressings or smaller items is on the refrigerator doors so they don't get lost in the back.

Fun Tip—We like to keep our beverage koozies/huggers/sleeves at the bottom of our refrigerator drawers. On those hot summer days, we like to keep our sodas cold as long as possible with already cool koozies.

A clean exterior on the refrigerator can have an immediate impact on the feel of your kitchen, as the magnets and pictures (while adorable!) tend to make kitchens appear cluttered. They could live on the side of the refrigerator facing a hallway. Consider attaching a metal baking sheet inside a cabinet door and use it for magnets and artwork. If you have limited space in your kitchen, the metal baking sheet can also store spices in magnetic tins. This leaves more space in cabinets or drawers and is visible and easy to access.

If you have kitchen items that you don't want to put in the dishwasher, or you don't have a dishwasher, a collapsible dish drainer with a spout is handy for small kitchens.

All kitchen cleaning supplies should be kept under the sink. A large plastic basket with a handle can provide sturdy storage for cleaning supplies and can be taken out easily to clean around the house. It is a great habit to clean the kitchen every night before you go to bed. It keeps the countertops clutter-free and makes breakfast prep the next morning so much easier and faster. If every family member pitches in to help, the task can be completed even quicker.

By putting everything away in zones, it helps you cook faster and more efficiently. Again, give everything a home where it is used the most. The goal is to have a clear and open counter space as much as possible, so you can come in and just start cooking.

Pantries

Pantries can be a small closet or large cabinet to a large walk-in pantry with many shelves. My daughter likes to see what the oldest thing is in our food pantry that has expired. I hate to throw food away, so I am not very good about going through the canned goods as often as I should!

An organized pantry has similar products stored together so food groups can have a designated home in your pantry, making them easy for each family member to find. If you are not sure where to put a food item, think of where they would zone the item in a grocery store. The pantry should be sorted and have *likes* together such as all the rice, canned goods, grains, beverages, etc. zoned together. It just needs to make sense to you and the household.

Set it up for food and cooking categories that suit your lifestyle (portable lunches, weeknight dinners, baking, etc.) The most often-used zones should be in easy reach, such as after-school snacks for kids. Label each zone, so when the family helps you put away groceries, they will know where everything belongs.

If your pantry is large enough, it will be a good place to store bulky or seldom-used utensils and small appliances. Put these in the corner or on the top shelf. Your most used cookware should remain in your kitchen. If possible, hang bulky utensils from hooks mounted on the wall. If you want to keep them in the kitchen but out of sight, hang them on the back of a cabinet door.

Matching containers on the shelves that fit your personal style will help make your pantry both functional and aesthetically pleasing. My favorite is the clear IDesign brand of pantry containers with integrated handles. They hold up well in a pantry and are easy to clean. These are appealing to clients with OCD and ADHD tendencies too, as it keeps the pantry shelves neatly organized, but you can still "see" what the containers hold. These containers come in various sizes and provide a sleek edge to pantry organization. The open, stackable bins match well and are great for small lightweight items like energy bars and individually packaged snacks, allowing quick, grab-and-go access. Turntables are great for pantry corners. Be sure and measure your pantry shelves before you buy any products. If your family likes cereal for breakfast, OXO Good Grips Container is a quality brand for pantry containers that seal in freshness and reduce the occurrence of pantry moths. They come in a variety of shapes and sizes for cereals, pasta, baking supplies, crackers, snacks, etc. If you have a large, busy family and go through cereal quickly, I would not recommend taking the time to put cereal in each container. If you have the time and really like the organized look in your pantry, then go for it.

A tiered shelf works well to store canned goods while providing easy access and keeping all cans in view. Group canned food by type (veggies, fruits, soups, etc.) and arrange in rows on the shelf. A clear floor in the pantry makes it appear larger, provides easy access to the enclosed spaces and allows for easy clean-up/sweeping. When items must be stored on the floor of the pantry, I recommend clear large, sturdy rectangular containers to keep these items clean and restrict them from migrating out onto the open floor space.

If you have the space to buy in bulk, that is okay, but if things start overflowing, then you need to set a limit. Create an area for products such as paper plates, napkins, plastic cups, and plastic ware in the same zone in your pantry. Only buy more when there is space available in that zone in the pantry.

Your party items are best kept on the top shelves. Stock a selection of plates, napkins, toothpicks, and trays are nice to keep on hand. The portable caddies are easy to grab when you want to eat outside and can be great places to store picnic utensils.

You will want a baking zone in your pantry. You can keep dry ingredients in clear, airtight containers that neatly stack and allow you to see when you need to restock. Place mixes, frostings, chocolate chips, and other ingredients next to these containers.

I have had the opportunity to work with couples who like to drink wine and entertain. In one kitchen, they had an entire shelf dedicated to wine glasses. All different types of styles and sizes were on this shelf. They used them often and they were beautiful but very unorganized. If you are a wine drinker, then you know how much you love to try different varieties of wine. When it was time to entertain, they would put them on display so everyone could see, taste and admire the different collections. I suggested they buy a liquor cabinet. I organized it with all the bottles stored neatly on the top shelves and the beautiful glasses organized on the next shelves. It was a nice addition to the kitchen.

One of the tasks that homeowners often underestimate is cleaning the pantry shelves. There are many foods, such as crackers, chips, fruits, cereal, and vinegar that have a short shelf life. When you buy in bulk, each product has its own shelf life, and at some point, these items will go stale. The shelf life varies depending on the item. The rule of thumb is that foods and beverages should be consumed within a year of purchase, but some will last longer than others. Many people are not willing to throw away food because they have not developed an established habit of throwing out expired foods.

Key Takeaways from This Chapter

- **Kitchen Cabinets**—Make sure to store *like* items in areas in the cabinets. Zone the kitchen for different tasks.
- **Coffee/Tea Breakfast Center**—Arrange the center in a visually appealing manner. Display items where they are convenient for the whole family.
- **Pantry**—Group *like* items together. Pitch expired food. Clean the shelves once a year. Zone the pantry like a grocery store.

I hope this chapter was helpful as you declutter your kitchen and pantry! In the next chapter, I will discuss breakfast nooks, kitchen eating areas, and dining rooms.

5

BREAKFAST NOOKS, KITCHEN EATING AREAS, AND DINING ROOMS

"Dinner is not what you do in the evening before something else. Dinner is the evening."

ART BUCHWALD

I know what you are thinking—those boring brown chairs and that hideous table with the yellow-flowered tablecloth, and those same old light fixtures. Why would anyone want to eat in this room anyway?

Well, you never have to worry about that again because I am here to help you with those breakfast nooks, kitchen eating areas, and dining rooms. You will learn everything you need to know about these rooms so you can create a fun place to eat, whether it be for your family or guests.

Having daily meals together as a family is a healthy habit for everyone. Statistics show that children who routinely eat with their parents are more successful in school, develop good social skills, build stronger communication skills, and have fewer drug abuse problems as teenagers, so having family meals is a win/win for everyone.

Another good family rule is no phones at the table. Everyone in the family should put their phones on the chargers during meal times. It is much healthier for children to learn how to have conversations and to not be texting each other while eating at the table.

Something fun to buy to keep close to your family table is a set of *Table Topics Conversation Cards*. There are some for couples, teens, and kids, and they can be a great way to enjoy your mealtimes!

Dining Rooms

Dining rooms can be used to seat many guests, entertain and for formal dinners.

Each home is different in this area. Some have formal dining areas with large China hutches and table seating for 12, and some are eating areas in the kitchen, breakfast nooks, or kitchen eating bars. You need to set this area up so it works best for you and your family.

If you want to keep a formal dining room, this is a good place to have a buffet, China hutch, or sideboard cabinet to keep your formal dishes or party items. It could also be used to store more of your seasonal items like candles or fragile items that you wouldn't want to store in the garage.

Some people also use the sideboard or buffet for their coffee/tea station. For convenience, I suggest the coffee/tea station be as close to your kitchen sink as possible.

Sometimes, the dining table becomes a catch-all. If you want to stop that from happening, clean it off and dress the table with a seasonal runner and centerpiece. Once it is "dressed," it is less tempting to become the dropping point and will be an attractive space when people enter your home.

Things to consider when organizing a dining room:

1. You want to make sure there is enough space for guests to be able to move around without bumping into one another.
2. You may want to have a special China cabinet or buffet for your special dishes.
3. Make your dining room feel warm and inviting by keeping it bright and light.
4. The light hanging from the ceiling should be at least 30 to 34 inches above the center of the table. For ceilings higher than 8 feet, add 3 inches for the hanging height per foot.

If you want to keep a formal dining room great. Be sure it has enough table space and chairs for when you have guests. If you never use it for dining, here are a few ideas. Since the dining area is usually right off the kitchen, it can also make a great family room, playroom, office, or craft room. Don't be bound by what the realtor called a particle room; make sure the space works for you!

ONLY EAT IN THE KITCHEN AND DINING AREAS. Don't eat in your bedroom unless you have a studio apartment, and then I would recommend a murphy bed with a desk. Eating anywhere else besides the kitchen or dining area leads to dirty dishes, glasses, crumbs, and uneaten food that may invite insects and pests all over the house.

Breakfast Nooks

"Knowledge is knowing a tomato is a fruit; wisdom is not putting it in a fruit salad." —Miles Kington

A breakfast nook in the kitchen is a cozy and intimate place where family members can gather to talk, read, play games, do puzzles and share a meal. It is also a great spot for casual entertaining.

Organizing a breakfast nook is all about the details. You want to make it a comfortable and cozy place for eating, but you also want to make it nice for hosting meals.

How should you clear clutter in breakfast nooks? The table should be kept clear and cleaned up after every meal.

Ideas for casual entertaining in the breakfast nook include:

1. Providing a buffet of fresh fruit, drinks, and munchies for your guests to help themselves while they are visiting.
2. Using the breakfast bar as a buffet to display appetizers, condiments, and party foods (cupcakes, cookies, etc.).
3. Have a family board game night in the breakfast nook.

Kitchen Eating Areas

A kitchen eating area can be a very informal location for eating. Since you spend so much time in your kitchen, you want to make it feel bright and comfortable.

Cleaning clutter in your kitchen eating areas is much easier than in your kitchen because you are less likely to have lots of dishes and food prep on display.

Here are a few ideas to get you started:

1. Make sure you have enough room for a dinette or table.
2. In our first house, we just had a small corner, and I wanted an eating area in the kitchen so I could keep an eye on our children while cooking. We put in a banquette with a small table. The corner bench would open, and it provided extra storage in the kitchen. It gave us much needed storage space, and with upholstery it brought both color and pattern to the room. It was very functional and created a cozy spot for meals and a place where our children could color, do crafts and homework too.

Make your kitchen eating area a comfortable and inviting space for your family and guests.

Key Takeaways from This Chapter

- **Breakfast Nooks**—Make sure your breakfast nook is comfortable and cozy.
- **Kitchen Eating Areas**—Great place for informal meals and snacks.
- **Dining Rooms**—Make sure it has enough seating for guests and large family gatherings.

In the next chapter, we will look at living rooms and family rooms.

6

LIVING ROOM AND FAMILY ROOMS

"The living room should be a place where we feel totally at ease."

TERENCE CONRAN

The living room is usually the very first room you see when entering a home and it is usually designed at its best. Are you a stylish type who loves to entertain at home, or just someone who likes a casual, comfortable living room? Figuring out your living room's style is important, as it will dictate what you need to put in your space and how you'll decorate it. As the room in the home that often serves as a place for friends and family to gather, your living room sets the tone for how guests perceive your home.

Formal or Informal?

Have you thought about whether to have a formal or informal living room? There are several design elements that we need to consider when making a decision. The size or dimensions of your floor space is one. Houses with larger floor plans can accommodate both a living room and a family room, setting up a formal living room is just perfect. However, some house designs come with limited space, which makes opting for an informal living room better.

Informal

The most common type of living room is the casual/informal type. This type of living room is a space where you can relax, play games, and mingle with friends. An informal living room is generally a place for the whole family. It should adapt to the needs of everyone. Because family activities are endless, furniture and fixtures are designed for comfort, relaxation and entertainment. It should be a casual space for the family members to interact.

Your informal living room can be attractive and multi-functional at the same time. A large leather couch can be positioned fronting the television accented with two bean bags on both sides to give that cozy feel. Your color hues don't have to match everything. I suggest a mix of sunny and earthy colors for a more homey yet carefree look. You can also fill idle spaces with geometric rugs and lazy chairs for popcorn and movie marathons. Just make sure to discard popcorn tubs right away to avoid clutter.

For this type of living room, an entertainment center with drawers or enclosures can keep it tidy after each activity. Most family activities can involve board games, puzzles and playing. Use the drawers to store materials after use. Always check those drawers at least every week for hidden clutter and put items in their respective places.

You may add a memorabilia or craft corner to create warm conversation pieces with relatives and friends. Customized cabinets with lots of compartments that can house art pieces can be a good fit for that corner. You can place valuable collections like breakables or rare decor on the upper shelf , picture frames at the center and small stackable boxes at the bottom for kids trinkets and craft materials.

Stackables always look neat on any shelf as they hide tiny items from sight. You can choose stackable boxes with inner dividers to keep small items from getting lost. They can also be color coded to easily distinguish which box contains what.

If you have an open concept home, be sure and define the space. Use a large rug to unite the seating group. Furniture arrangement can also divide the room into different activities. For example a sofa and chairs in front of a fireplace or window can encourage conversation.

I really like items and products that are versatile. Only one function is not enough! Though furniture or storage products often serve a single purpose, it's more worth the investment if it can meet more than one. I find it challenging to figure out how to make the most of storage spaces, and I try to purchase products that can help reach that goal. For example, I need an ottoman in my living room. I just don't want something to put my feet on while resting in a chair. I also want a place to store my blankets. So, I will always look for furniture pieces like end tables and coffee tables that can also store things. I don't think you can ever have enough convenient storage, even in large homes!

Formal

A formal living room is designed to have a more sophisticated feel. As it is called, this area has all the air of elegance and is often used for entertaining guests on special occasions that require formality. In western tradition, a formal living room is not a common place for everyday fun and is always kept in style.

The formal living room is like a gallery of impressive finds. Expensive glass pieces and a collection of rare decors can be found in every corner complementing the luxury sofa. You can hang several paintings on your center wall that go with the theme of your living room and choose an eye-catching center table to complete your interior design. And it is absolutely not a place for clutter.

My grandparents had a grand room or a formal living room that was beautiful. The secret? We were taught not to bring food in that room at any cost. Growing up, we kept our hands off any items with value like the tall vietnamese triple jar set that sat near the hallway and toys were not allowed in that room. Anyone who brought any kind of food or toys in the grand room would have to feed the rabbits in the backyard for a week as punishment. We helped dust table tops and couches like there were visitors coming everyday. Up to this day we treated the grand room with high regard, the way we respected elders. Even after my grandparents were gone, the grand room still stood the way it was and was used for formal functions and special holidays.

So if you decide to keep a formal living room in your home, you should have a family room for carefree fun and relaxation to keep your formal room clutter free at all times.

Family Room and/or Informal Living Rooms

Family rooms have multiple functions. From chit-chats to playing musical instruments, the room serves as a place where you make happy memories. Everything can happen around here making it hard to declutter and organize. Worse, all sorts of electronic gadgets and cable wires can be found everywhere.

It requires a lot of time and effort to get things done. Picking up things from the floor can really be so stressful that sometimes you feel like never doing it at all. To make it easy for you, start from the simplest tasks. Your teenage gamer might have left his Ipad on the couch with a charger still stuck in it, and Jamie's VR glasses sitting on the rug. You can gather these gadgets on one table for them to pick up so you can go ahead and scan the room for other messes.

Remove all items that don't belong in the family room. You might have done your nails in front of the television or might have forgotten that you left a pot holder beside the telephone when your friend called. The nail polish bottle and the pot holder obviously should not be in the living room so you need to pick them up as soon as you remember.

The Tidy Rule-*If it takes fewer than two minutes to put an item back in it's "home," do it now, and it will save a lot more time later when you go looking for the item!*

More often, most of the clutter in your family room or living room doesn't even belong in there in the first place. Old magazines and books can often take up a lot of space. You sometimes keep an old broken lamp behind the new one because you think you will get it fixed. But all of them need to go to freshen up those spaces. Also check on things you happen to bring into the room at one point. It can be anything from a dust cloth, a water bottle, cosmetics, clothes and shoes. All these items have a place and it's certainly not the family room.

Shoes need to go back to the shoe rack. Other things that don't belong to the room should be returned to their places as well. Make it a habit to remember everything you've brought into the family room by chance. That way it should also be your habit to put them back in their respective places. Set this example for your family members to follow. And you'll be surprised to find your home more breathable than ever.

In designing your family room, choosing multi function or dual function furniture and fixtures play a big role in your home organizing tasks. Storage sofas are a hit. Most home designers recommend these furniture to create more open spaces. You can never have enough storage! These sofas are sometimes designed with pull-out compartments or a collapsible backrest to reveal the storage. These are smart choices for modern living.

Organize the Books and Movies

The living space is a really good area to have a small bookcase or other shelving units. There are many things that can pile up in your living space, and it can look like a mess in no time. You need to have a place to put a lot of these items, including the movies and books, to keep them out of the way. Using a bookcase or built-in cabinets work nicely.

You can arrange the movies in alphabetical order by movie title. This helps you choose movies easily for future viewing. Books can also be arranged by categories and size. Children's books should be stacked on a lower shelf for easy access. You may just want to place the movies on one shelf and the books on another. You don't have to get too technical here with the organization; just make sure everything gets placed nicely on the shelves or in cabinets rather than scattered all over the room.

Separate Into Different Areas

If you use the family room or informal living room for more than one activity, take the time to separate the room into those areas. For example, if your family likes to socialize in the living space, make sure there are plenty of chairs present for everyone to be comfortable. Perhaps have a little storage nook for some blankets if you want to sit down and watch a show together. You could set up a little table for puzzles, games to play or have some special chairs for playing video games.

Each family uses their living spaces in different ways, and the method you use for organizing will vary depending on your own particular uses. But when you organize the room based on uses, it becomes much easier to keep everything in its place.

Clean Off the End Tables and Entertainment System

You will need to spend some time organizing and dusting your furniture in the living room. Let's start with the end tables. Lots of items can build up when it comes to your end tables. Go through and get rid of any extra papers and items that are cluttering up the end table, whether they are on top or in the drawer. Throw away anything that you no longer need. Only keep a few necessities inside the drawer of the end table and get it cleared off as much as possible. Once the end table is cleared, you can dust off the top and all the sides.

The entertainment system is the next thing to work on. If you have pictures put on top, take time to switch them out to provide updated options and dust them off before reorganizing. Dust off all the entertainment units, such as TVs and stereos, and be sure everything is in working order. Go through all the remotes and be sure they are working and that you still have the device that they go with. Remotes put on a tray on a coffee or end table is a good way to keep them all together.

If you keep any shelving in your living space, take time to clean these off as well. Often when we are in a hurry, we will just throw random objects onto the shelves and hope we can worry about them later. Get rid of all this junk, either by throwing it away or putting it in its right place. Next, remove even the things that belong on the shelves so you can do a thorough job of dusting, before reorganizing and making it all look tidy.

Dust off and organize anything else that may be in the living room, whether it is a coffee table or something else. Everything should be clear of clutter when you are done, and the whole room can be organized and cleaned.

Get a Magazine Rack

Magazines, books and papers can quickly pile up in your home. You may not have time to read them at one time and will set them aside to finish up later. Unfortunately, life gets in the way, and after several months, you can accumulate lots of magazines and books lying all over the room. A good place to store these is in a magazine rack.

There are a lot of racks that you can choose from; go for one that is sturdy and will be easy to fit in your room. Go through all the catalogs and magazines and throw away all that you have already read or that you don't believe you will finish. If there is an article you want to keep, just snap a photo of it and get rid of the magazine. In addition, only keep one or two books out in the living room at a time; you won't have time to read more than that anyway, and you can just put the rest away on a shelf. You can always switch them out later.

Any time you bring out a new book or receive a new magazine in the mail, you can place it in the magazine rack so it is ready whenever you are. Just make sure to clean out the magazine rack at least a few times each year. Otherwise, it will become overcrowded with items you aren't using, and you will start making a mess again.

Dust and Wash Windows

Once you have cleared out the rest of the room, take some time to clean the windows. Be sure the curtains are clean and updated. New curtains can change the entire feel of a room. If they are dusty, take them down and shake them outside or put them in the clothes dryer. If they are formal drapes, have them professionally cleaned at least once a year.

Vacuum

Before leaving the room, make sure to do a thorough vacuum job. By cleaning off all the other things in the room—from the shelves to moving things around—you will leave quite a bit of a mess on the floor, so vacuum the floor last. You should also move some of the furniture around so you can get the dirt and grime, and remove the cushions from the couch to get everything that has fallen in between there. You will be amazed at how great the room feels once it is clean and decluttered, and how more comfortable the couch feels after vacuuming. If you keep items off the floor and put them in their places, you will find cleaning much easier and faster.

The living space is an important room in your home. It is the place where you get to spend a lot of time with your family, socializing, and especially relaxing. You will want to take special precautions to make this place look amazing so it can still allow for family bonding time without becoming a mess again. With the help of these tips, and maintaining the hard work you are doing, you will find it easier to keep the living space feeling cozy and inviting.

Key Takeaways from This Chapter

- This chapter covered the different styles of living rooms: formal and informal and family rooms.
- Since the family spaces can gather a mixture of items, always remember: The Tidy Rule-*If it takes fewer than two minutes to put an item back in it's "home," do it now, and it will save a lot more time later when you go looking for the item!*

In the next chapter, you will learn how to organize your bedrooms, bathrooms, and closets for adults.

7

ADULT BEDROOMS, BATHROOMS AND CLOSETS

"The sole purpose of the bedroom is to melt away any stressors."

JONATHAN SCOTT

How do you feel whenever you walk into your bedroom or bathroom? Tired, overwhelmed, and frustrated from the clutter that has accumulated over the years? Is it time to change the look and feel of your space?

In this chapter, we will go over how to organize your bedroom, bathroom, and closet spaces. The goal will be to help get rid of clothes no longer worn and items no longer used and organize the spaces for a relaxing retreat!

Bedroom

The main bedroom should provide a calm retreat every night. Get rid of anything that isn't related to relaxation, romance, sleeping, or dressing. Other items need to go in the closet—no work or other unfinished projects or papers should be allowed. I know the dresser can become another cluttered catch-all, but try to put items away and out of the bedroom as soon as possible.

If you are having any trouble falling or staying asleep, maybe it is time to get the electronics out of your bedroom. Some people decide to eliminate TVs and other electronic equipment from the bedroom. It's a good way to prime your bedroom for relaxation. Even the colors in your bedroom can make a difference. A study from Sleep.org, found that the color blue can lead to a better night's sleep. Blues are calming and relaxing and, therefore, lower your blood pressure. While blue is the most relaxing, other cool tones such as grays, neutrals, and paints with gray or blue undertones can also help you sleep longer.

Your bedside table should hold items used just before you go to sleep. Clear the clutter and stylishly organize only what you need. The top of the table should be even with the top of the mattress to fit the bed. A few inches above or below is okay too. If it is more than 24 inches from the wall, you could hit your legs when you get out of bed, so it shouldn't be a large nightstand. If the tabletop is small, a wall-mounted lamp helps save space.

If you are in need of more storage, I would recommend getting a nightstand with drawers instead of just a table. Small drawer dividers could separate small items in a top drawer (pens, earplugs, lip balm, hand cream, tissues, etc.). It is easy for this area to become a junk catch-all too, so to prevent that, stick with just the items you need at night. If you want to keep your glasses, etc. on the tabletop, a cute tray will give a less cluttered look. A larger drawer could hold your "brain drain" notebook, overnight items, reading material, glasses, etc.

Extra storage can be obtained on the sides of your bed by a hanging organizer that is anchored between the mattress and box springs. It can hold books, glasses, remotes, etc.

Drawer dividers for dresser drawers can help organize folded clothes, socks and underwear. Expandable drawer dividers work well to divide clothes stored in drawers. If space is an issue, I suggest a tall chest to help with more storage. If you have a tall chest, be sure and anchor it to the wall to prevent falling.

Still need more storage space? The horizontal space under the beds can also be utilized for much-needed storage. Try putting risers on the legs of your bed to give it a small lift. My favorite under-bed storage is the clear plastic containers on rollers with a middle hinge on the lid. The hinge is really nice and makes it so you don't have to take the container all the way out to open the lid and get to something. This is a great place for a variety of items, such as off-season clothes, shoes, books, keepsakes, etc.

Make up the bed each morning. That could just mean pulling the sheets and comforters to the top of the bed. It makes your room appear more organized all day and going to bed at night much more relaxing.

You should change or wash your bedsheets and pillowcases weekly, meaning anything touching your skin. This eliminates dust mites that can pose a risk of acquiring allergies. It removes odor caused by sweat, and clean bedding is softer and more comfortable. Bulky comforters do not need to be washed as frequently. If they are the washable kind, they can be taken to the extra-large washing machines at a laundromat during spring cleaning or whenever needed. I made the mistake of trying to wash my bulky comforter in my regular size washing machine, and it was too big, and the washing machine ripped my comforter!

Linen Closets

Towels, sheet sets and extra pillows and blankets should be stored in a linen closet.

This tip I actually got from a client. She had taken her set of folded sheets and put each set in one of the pillowcases. That way, the flat sheet, fitted sheet, and pillowcases were all together. We labeled the closet shelves with size and room, for example: Twin Set for the Guest room, King Set for the Main Bedroom, Queen Set for Sam's Room, etc. Blankets and comforters can then be put on the next shelf with size labels. If linen closet space is limited, try putting the blankets and comforters in vacuum storage bags to minimize the space they consume.

Your linen closet should be home to extra linens for the guest room, extra blankets, your blow-up mattress, etc. I recommend only two sets of sheets for a guest bed, so one can be ready to go on the bed on laundry day. Since my guest bed is not used very often, I only have the following on the bed: mattress pad, pillows, and bedspread or comforter. That way, when I know guests are arriving soon, I can put on the fresh sheets and pillowcases from the closet.

Closets

If you create a routine of hanging up your daily clothes or putting them in the dirty clothes hamper when you come home, this habit will keep clothes clutter at a minimum. We all have clothes that we only wore for a couple hours and may wear the next day. Put those on a hook in the closet so they are easy to grab when you get dressed in the morning. One client did this, but she got carried away with too many clothes she said she was going to wear again. It was taking up an entire bedroom chair. She just didn't want to take the time to hang them back up. Only keep one hook of wear-again clothes and hang the rest back up or put them in the dirty clothes hamper to cut down on the clothes clutter.

If you have a shelf height that isn't working for you... change it! This goes for closets, kitchen cabinets, pantries, bookshelves, media units, medicine cabinets, and refrigerator shelves too! I had a client with three closets in their home that were not working for them. They had very high ceilings, even in the closets. At the consultation, I suggested moving both the rods/shelf up because his clothes were hitting the floor. By the time I had seen the entire house, we had a long list for a handyman that he hired to get all the closet shelves adjusted and ready for us to organize.

If your closet only has one rod and shelf, and you need more room to hang clothes, I suggest having a second rod put in and raising the existing rod. This can be a permanent change, or, if you are in an apartment, a temporary rod addition like the ones that hang from the current rod works well too. If you don't have a lot of space for a dresser, hanging closet organizers can help. These are hung from the closet rod. They can be narrow and used for shoes or wider for sweaters, pants, etc.

Many Professional Organizers will recommend the flocked hangers to hang clothes because they are thin and save space on the clothing rod, hold clothes well without slippage, and create a sleek look to the hanging clothes. The light-colored ones will not show dust as readily as the black ones. You can add clips to these flocked hangers to use for hanging skirts or shorts. Another option for skirts and shorts is to use plastic clip hangers, depending on your preference. But, if you just like to yank your clothes down, I would NOT recommend the flocked hangers because they may get caught, and you could rip your clothes. If you like to yank and go as I do, I suggest getting all the same color plastic hangers. Just having them all the same color will still give your closet a nice look.

If you go to the dry cleaners a lot, do not leave your clothes in the plastic bags. The chemicals can harm the garments over time. Take all the clothes off the paper hangers, put them on your plastic or flocked hangers, and throw the bags away. Most dry cleaners will recycle your paper/wire hangers.

While getting dressed, after you take a garment off the hanger, put the hanger at the end of the rod and closest to the door. Teach your entire family to do this. When you get ready to do laundry, you can just grab the hangers and not have to go through the entire closet looking for hangers for the clean clothes.

On your shelves above the rods, use shelf dividers to keep sweaters or pants from tumbling. They can help contain your purses, bags, and stacks of folded clothes too. Bubble wrap or packing paper can be stuffed into purses so they hold their shape and look nice on the shelves.

Hats can take a lot of room on a shelf. If you have wall space, hang the hats on hooks on the wall inside your closet. If you live in an apartment, 3M Command Strip hooks are your friend!

Hanging items together and sorting them by color will allow you to match outfits with ease. The closet should be arranged by category first. For example, all jeans together, all shirts together, suits together, dresses together, etc. The next sort should be all short sleeve knit shirts together, then long sleeve knit shirts, etc. Within each category, arrange by color from white all through the color wheel to black. This will help you see what duplicates you have. Do you really need 11 gray t-shirts? If you have room, keep a box in the closet for clothes that are out of style, don't fit anymore, etc. When it is full, put the box in your car and drop it off at a donation center. This will give you more room to keep your wardrobe updated and in style.

Clear plastic sweater boxes are great for closet storage when you need to "see" the items stored on the upper shelves. A little more expensive option would be to use matching baskets or boxes for storage on the upper closet shelves. This will give a polished look to the closet when you don't need to "see" what is in the boxes (you still need to label them with the contents).

Assign a specific purpose for each box such as all your clutch purses or wallets in one box.

Accessories need room to hang so items can live together. Hangers for ties, belts, and scarves can keep these accessories organized and set thresholds on how many to keep.

If you love boots, inexpensive swim noodles can be cut to fit and may be used for stuffing into tall boots so they hold their shape. Out-of-season boots and shoes can be stored in lidded boot boxes on the upper shelves to protect them from dust during the off-season.

If you have a lot of shoes, an inexpensive, stackable shoe shelf on the floor of your closet can double your shelf space. If you have deep shelves, you can arrange them from heel to toe, or one behind the other so you only see one shoe but both are together for easy access.

If you have lots of necklaces, small 3M Command hooks are a great way to hold a lot of necklaces! Hanging them really helps keep them from getting tangled and allows you to see what you have that goes with the outfit you have selected. Since I have a narrow walk-in closet and wanted to keep the dust off my jewelry, we installed a flush to the wall metal gun safe that fit between the wall studs. I took the small clear 3M Command hooks and stuck them to the back of the metal cabinet and hung up all my costume jewelry. I also have a jewelry cabinet that hangs on the wall (they make these to hang on the back of a door too). That is where I store my earrings and rings. A great item to have in your jewelry area is a small box labeled "Lost and Found." So many times we lose one earring or the back of an earring, etc. Put the lost items in your lost and found box, so when you do find the other earring, you know where to match them up again!

If you have room and access to another bedroom closet, keep only current season clothing in your bedroom closet. Changing seasons is a good time to see what you have and have not worn. If you haven't worn it in a year, time to donate. Pull out all the off-season clothes by category, for example, all your heavy sweaters, and decide what you are keeping. For the ones you do keep, put them in another bedroom closet, but be sure they are clean. Dirty clothes put in storage can start to smell and can attract pests. If you start to run out of room in the drawers or hanging spaces, it is time to purge. The average person wears only 20% of their clothes 80% of the time. That is why, when there is a change in season, it is a good time to donate out of style or unwanted items.

Your space defines how much you can own! To prevent your items from taking over your closet, decide how much space you want to allocate to a particular item, and then stick with it! We call this a threshold that cannot be crossed. As an example, I have one drawer in my dresser that I've allocated to sweaters. I don't allow myself to own any more sweaters than can fit in that drawer. If I buy a new sweater, but the drawer is full, I have to get rid of an existing sweater. I can't put it in another drawer or on a shelf in the closet. It's the same with my shoes. If my shoe shelf is full, I can't buy a new pair of shoes unless I get rid of a pair. By creating limits for myself and my family members, I ensure that we continue to live comfortably within our thresholds.

One client had so many clothes, shoes, purses, etc. that she was paying monthly for a 10 x 12 storage unit. When we helped her open all the boxes and bags and went through the clothes in the storage unit, she ended up with at least six trips with her SUV full of clothes to the donation center. If you can take the time to go through your items, you may end up saving money and not having to pay monthly for a storage unit. Storage units should only be used as a temporary storage solution. Maybe during a move or helping parents downsize, etc. If you have had the unit for more than a year, I highly recommend taking a weekend and going through your items and getting rid of what you haven't missed in over a year.

Travel

If you have the room, keep your luggage on the top shelf of your closet. They usually nest and are handy to bring down when you need to start packing.

When packing for a trip, check the weather in your destination first. Remember that things can always be layered with a jacket if it gets too cold, so try not to overpack.

My husband and I each have travel toiletry organizer bags that we keep in our overnight bags. They rarely get unpacked. We keep it full of all our travel needs such as (travel size) toothpaste, soap, shampoo, conditioner, deodorant, and razors. That way, we know all we have to do is add our vitamins and replace anything that has run out. Other very helpful items to keep in your toiletry bag include eyeglass repair, sewing, and first aid kits. That way, you are prepared for the unexpected. Within the toiletry bags, we store liquid toiletries in clear plastic bags. This will keep them safe from spills and make them easy to see for both you and the TSA!

I recommend packing the weekend before any trip. Generally, you will have more time and are calmer at that time. If there are things you need, you'll have time to purchase them. Keep a list of items you need to bring to ensure you never leave without the essentials, like medications, passport, etc. Tip: Create a digital version on your phone so you can reference and update it when needed.

I usually pull tops and bottoms from the closet and make an outfit for every day I will be gone, plus one in case I spill something on it or the weather changes. Try to plan full outfits in advance to be sure you have pieces that will work together and are comfortable. If you haven't worn them in a while, try the set on to be sure everything still fits. If you stick with one color pallet, this also helps with shoes and jewelry. For example, put together everything that goes with black pants and black shoes—tops can be gray, pink, royal blue, etc.

If you are not using a travel agent, create an itinerary with dates from the necessary travel documents with general information like dates/times, etc. This can also be done by printing out your hotel reservations. That way, if you are driving, you have the address of the next hotel you will be staying at.

If you have places you want to see, you can make notes for each day, working your way from morning until night. Lastly, don't forget to proofread and double-check your documents. This would have really helped us on a return trip from Maui. We thought we were flying out at 11AM. After checking out of the hotel and returning our rental car, we walked up to the ticket counter at the airport. They looked at us and said that we were too early to check-in for the 11PM flight. We rented another car and enjoyed some more time on the island (it was OK, it was Maui!) but it would have been a much more relaxing breakfast if we had double-checked the tickets!

If you are traveling to another country, make a copy of your birth certificate and copy of your passport and keep them in your suitcase. If you lose your passport, you will still have a backup.

Ziploc bags are handy for small clothes items too. For example, children's socks and underwear can be stored in a Ziploc bag, and then placed in a suitcase.

Put shoes in plastic grocery bags. One shoe in each bag, then they can be stuffed along the edge of the suitcase and won't get your clothes dirty. They also won't take up as much room. Make sure to pack a few extra plastic grocery bags for wet clothes, such as swimsuits, in case they don't have time to dry before having to pack for your departure. The plastic bags are also handy to store dirty clothes until you get home.

Carry-On Luggage

In your airplane or cruise ship carry-on bag, bring your prescription medicines, cameras, laptops, and any expensive jewelry onboard with you. It is also a good idea to have one change of underwear for each family member in case your luggage has issues. This happened to us on a flight home from Mexico. They overbooked the flight and offered free round-trip tickets for each member of our family. Since I love a deal and love to travel, we spent one night in Dallas (airline paid for the hotel and transportation to and from the airport), but our luggage was already on its way home, so all we had were our carry-on bags. The airline gave us some toothpaste and toothbrushes, but that was about it. Makes you realize what is really important in life and how you can live with much less.

Safety Tip: We carry the wedge-shaped rubber door stops in our luggage to put in front of the door on the floor before we go to bed in hotel rooms, Airbnbs, etc. You never know who has the key to your room or rental house! Just recently I heard about two couples traveling together, and they rented a 2-bedroom VRBO in Tennessee. The second morning they woke up, they discovered they had been robbed. The list of things missing was long, including rental cars, computers, phones, purses, and wallets. While talking to the police, they found out that this was not the first time this had happened at that address! Be sure and check the reviews for a property on several websites; some websites allow the owners to delete negative reviews.

Bathroom

As with every room, start with S.P.A.C.E. Refer back to Chapter 1 for details.

Acrylic drawer organizers are great for organizing small items in bathroom drawers. These are good for separating cosmetics, as they come in a variety of shapes and sizes for bathroom drawers. Shallow ones for the top drawers and deep ones for the deeper drawers. Most items living on your countertop should be moved into drawers and cabinets. Then, overflow products and lesser-used products could be moved into bathroom closets or cabinets. Containers with lids allow you to contain items together and stack the containers on deep closet shelves. Simply label each container to identify the contents (cold and sinus meds; first aid kit; shaving; body lotions; etc.). The metal or plastic pull-out drawer units below bathroom sinks are handy. They are also easy to label, with the labels facing up so it is easy to see when you open the cabinet door and pull out the drawer.

It is easy to allow toiletries to pile up at the back of your bathroom drawers. Make-up does have expiration dates. Take out all your make-up and pitch any expired products. Once the package is open, it can be a breeding ground for bacteria. Also, both over-the-counter medications and prescriptions have expiration dates. Check dates and dispose of old products every six months. Expired medicines you no longer need should not be tossed in the trash or flushed down the toilet because it can create contamination. Safely dispose of them by taking them to a nearby drug store. Be sure to blacken out your personal information on the container label before discarding.

When additional storage space is needed, you could also consider adding a cabinet above the toilet to house items such as extra toilet paper, feminine products, air fresheners, etc.

If you need more space but only have the counter, you can use clear apothecary jars to store small items like q-tips, cotton balls, etc. to make it look pretty and functional.

Tip: If you are like me and use hairspray, you probably have some overspray spots on the counter, wall, or floor. Dip a cloth rag in rubbing alcohol and clean the area. This works great if you don't want to let the hairspray build up over time. Don't do like I did and let it build up on the floor! I had to take a plastic scraper to get the hairspray off my tile floor. Can we all say *ewwwww!*

Key Takeaways from This Chapter

- **Bedroom**—Your bedroom is your retreat. It should be a peaceful place where you can relax and rejuvenate at the end of the day.
- **Bathroom**—Keep the bathroom organized and clean. You use it daily and will appreciate it more if everything is quick and easy to find.

The next chapter will help us get organized in children's and teens' bedrooms and bathrooms.

8

CHILDREN AND TEEN BEDROOMS AND BATHROOMS

"Each day of our lives we make deposits in the memory banks of our children."

CHARLES R. SWINDOLL

I have learned a lot about being prepared. Some parents meet you at a playdate at the park with their kids, carrying their lunch, hats, sunscreen, toys, and even a change of clothes for each child. I was often doing great if each child was fully dressed; I had a stroller in the car and wasn't more than 10 minutes late!

Preparation is key to being organized and successful. I have learned that getting things ready the night before makes it much easier, especially since I am not a morning person. My day runs so much smoother if I am not rushing around trying to be on time. Planning can really take a lot of stress out of your life!

The entire family needs to be involved in keeping an organized home. Children should have chores (age-appropriate). When I asked my 4 year old niece what it meant to organize her response was - *To put all your things in the right spot!* Here are a few examples of chores -Ages 2 and 3 - Pick up toys/books, Help make bed, Help feed pets. Ages 4 and 5 - Help with cooking and set the table, water houseplants. Ages 6 to 8-Take care of pets, take out trash, vacuum, make their bed every day and so on. The older they get the more responsibilities they should have. Our job as parents is to create responsible, caring adults.

Bedrooms

Kids need to keep their own areas organized because they have a lot of stuff, and it's hard for anyone else to keep track of it for them. When they make their beds every morning, it keeps the room neater and makes them feel more grown up. They live in the house too, and they must learn these skills for when they have a home of their own. If they have to share a bedroom and/or bathroom, being organized is even more important.

We used to tell our kids that you have to work to eat, so twice a day, they needed to pick up toys and reset their rooms. Depending on their age, it didn't mean that everything was perfect and in its place. It was more about getting stuff off the floor and back into the bins. Before lunch and dinner, we would have a room inspection, and if the room passed, they could go wash their hands and get ready for meal time. Since they were usually hungry, it gave them an incentive to get their rooms picked up quickly!

If you have a playroom, remove most of the toys from the bedroom and place them in the playroom. Add a desk with a chair and bookshelf to the bedroom to make it a haven of quiet reading, studying, and sleeping. If your child has ADD, ADHD or autism, they may have trouble with time. A digital clock often doesn't work for them. They need to see how time changes, so I highly recommend putting analog clocks in their rooms to tell time. Some children struggle to make transitions for example whether it is time to do homework or go to bed, etc. A helpful website that covers this issue in detail is www.timetimer.com.

Kids' Papers and Keepsakes

Keepsakes—Some families have lots (and I mean *lots*) of keepsakes or memorabilia. I had one client that had twin girls. When I helped organize their home, the girls were in junior high school. The mom had collected every piece of paper that the girls had ever written on (and by writing on, I mean a 2-line scribble at age 1 was included!). She even kept a bank document because one of the girls (at 4 years old) had drawn a picture of... not sure, maybe she is an upcoming Picasso? on the back of the document while they were waiting at the bank. After many years of keeping almost all the girls' school papers, art projects, etc. she was running out of storage space.

My recommendation on kids' papers is important because they are abundant and can take over counters, bedrooms, and furniture in no time! The amount of paper your child will bring home will grow as they go through elementary school, so it's helpful to develop a system early. The system for kids' papers is really simple if you resist the urge to deal with it daily.

All papers that do not require immediate action should go into a temporary holding spot accessible for each child so they can drop papers in it each day. This can be a large, plastic, clear tub or clear stackable drawers. Make sure to have a large drawer for each child and put their name on the front. Put all their school papers, art, awards, birthday cards, etc. in this container.

Keep the stackable drawers in a handy spot so the items get into the container quickly, such as the garage or entryway. At the end of the school year, go through the entire tote with the child and only keep the best from that year. This will help you avoid keeping everything because you will probably see a lot of similar work. Take what you have decided to keep and put it in a tote kept on the top shelf of their closet with their name. It may only end up being a folder so you can keep several years in one tote. The original stackable drawers are kept handy and ready for the next school year.

Once you have the entire year, separate into categories when putting in the closet tote:

Artwork—Save only the very best. Take a digital picture of your child with any really large or three-dimensional artwork (like dioramas, costumes, etc.), and then discard the bulky items.

Everyday papers—Worksheets, tests, handwriting exercises, essays, etc. go here. From this pile, save only the papers that are memorable, like essays about the family, current events, the ones your child is most proud of, etc. When considering what to keep, think about what would be interesting for your child to read about themselves in 25 years.

Ribbons, certificates—Keep only those that the child is really proud of. They may not care about the ribbon if every child got the same one!

Once they get into high school, keep science and speech meet ribbons/certificates, civic awards, state tests, report cards, volunteer hours, etc. that can be used when applying for college. They can also be used to build a resume, apply for scholarships, complete college applications, fill out job applications, etc. Anything that shows leadership qualities or community service can help your child stand out from the crowd on their applications.

If you have room, you can keep stories they have written in case they want to publish a book someday. If you are having a hard time getting rid of something, take a digital picture of it. Keeping it digitally takes up a lot less space, and many times makes them faster to find! Keep a file on your computer that is labeled "keepsakes" for each family member and the date it was created.

We have a family funny book. When the children were young I wanted to remember the funny things they did and said. I encourage you to create a file on your computer. Each entry in the file has the child's name and the month and year it happened. For example - When my granddaughter was 4 years old and we were talking about something and she looked at me and said "That is hilarious!" and I said yes it is! She then looked at me and said, "What is hilarious?" So I said, "You are!". When you need a good laugh it is so much fun to go back and read the stories. Our book has continued through all our children and now grandchildren.

Nursery—Diaper pails are sources of home odor. To prevent the smell, be sure to empty regularly. Clean the inside every month, including the underside of the lid. A little baking soda at the bottom of the container can absorb odors between cleanings. Keep the lid on to contain smells too.

Closet—Most children's closets need two rods: taller and lower that can be adjusted as they grow. If you don't want to do anything permanent, then the adjustable hanging rods that hang from the current rod work well too.

Bathrooms

Always allocate your facial tissue, toilet paper, cleaning supplies, cleaning rags/sponges, etc. to your various bathrooms. This will make it quick and easy to clean those areas and distribute your bulky items to the areas they are used. Clear the countertop in the bathroom used by all your guests by utilizing the space under the sink for storage. You can even get a shower curtain liner with pockets to hold some children's toys and keep them organized yet out of sight if you also use that bathroom for guests.

A small hanging mesh basket for toys in the bathroom keeps a child occupied and entertained while in the tub.

Children's bathroom cabinets may need childproof locks until they are older. That way, you can keep the bathroom cleaning supplies under the sink without fear of them digging into it.

Planning for more children? I find that families with children tend to feel like they need to keep everything if they are planning on having more. The easiest way to handle this is to have several clear plastic bins labeled: Outgrown Clothes, Shoes and Outgrown Toys. Once these bins are full, go through the clothes in a sunlit area and check for stains and holes. If the clothes pass the test, put them in a bin with a label of the size range, then place them up on a high shelf for long-term storage. The rest of the items can be tossed or donated. Only keep the toys with all the pieces and that are in good shape. Put an age range on the label on each toy bin. Only keep the toys that you know they really liked and played with. Again, the others can be tossed or donated. This also goes for children's books, games, and puzzles.

If you don't plan on having more children, start donating whatever they outgrow, both toys and clothes. I know you think you will be a grandparent someday, but that's a long time to hang onto toys that your grandchildren may never play with. Maybe keep some items if someone special made them for your child, but only if you have the storage space. If it gets hard to part with, again, take a picture of the clothes or toys and donate the actual item to someone who could use it.

NOT a fun Tip, but a time saver! We all know children don't realize how sick they are sometimes until it is too late. Keep a plastic bowl or basin under their beds close to the headboard, so when they have to get up in the middle of the night to vomit, they can grab the bowl. Believe me, it will save you lots of time cleaning!

Key Takeaways from This Chapter

- Kids should be taught how to do chores at an early age. The earlier you start the easier it will be to continue through the teen years.
- The key to a good morning is to prepare the night before!
- Kids need to understand the importance of keeping their rooms clean and tidy.
- Keep the cleaning supplies for the bathroom under the sink but be sure and use child proof locks.

In the next chapter, we will focus on playrooms/areas, game rooms, and home theaters.

9

PLAYROOMS/AREAS, GAME ROOMS AND HOME THEATERS

"For every minute spent organizing, an hour is earned."

BENJAMIN FRANKLIN

Have you ever asked yourself how to arrange your playroom, game room, or home theater so you can have the best experience? It's important to think about what you want it for. Often, when I work with clients in these areas, we talk about how they would like the space organized. We discuss what they have done before and the reasons for those decisions.

Playrooms/Areas

This does not have to be an entire room. It can even be a play area under the stairs or in a closet. My playroom growing up was a small closet off the living room and I loved it. I could fit a child-size table and two chairs, some books, a few toys, and I even had room for at least one friend.

If the play space is small, using the vertical wall space for storage works great with a cube system like the IKEA Trofast to keep toys organized. At the end of each day, have the child put away the toys in their proper homes, and the space should be cleared of toys each night.

Cube storage organizers are a great way to store toys in bins. The system can grow with your children. I suggest getting the cube size to hold bins that are at least 13 inches by 15 inches. You can add doors, drawers, and various cube inserts to contain small items. Each cube should be labeled so the toys find their way back to their proper homes. The cube inserts can also be used to set thresholds for toy accumulation and clutter. For example, if the cube for balls is full, then no more balls can be added unless some are donated; all the balls must fit into one cube. Then, consider a rule that only two cubes of toys can be out at one time. This helps control clutter and chaos, allows more room for imaginative play in the space, and makes clean-up a lot easier.

I am not a fan of toy boxes unless it is for large toys because so many small toys get lost at the bottom. We have a toy box that is also a bench, so it's not really deep and works nicely for larger stuffed animals, plus there's the added versatility of being a place for your child to sit and play. A better way to store toys in a playroom is to put them in small bins sorted by different types of toys and then label the bins. We will talk more about labels later.

Cube storage organizers are versatile too. It can be put on the wall vertically if not a lot of floor space, or the two wide cube storages can lay on their side to hold bins and or books. The child can sit on top. This makes it a great place to read books, do puzzles; again, it is versatile. The bins are also nice because, as the child grows older, you can update the bin to match their room. If floor space is not limited, I suggest at least four cubes high and three cubes wide.

You have to be very careful with stuffed animals because they tend to multiply in the night when no one is looking! The mesh corner nets come in several sizes and can be hung in the corner of the room to store stuffed animals and keep them off the floor.

I suggest an adjustable child-size table and chairs. The legs of both the chairs and table can slide up or down, so they are adjustable as your children grow.

Seems like every child has Legos or some type of building blocks. These are great for the bins.

Another great thing for kids is rotating toys in and out of the playroom. If you have a closet nearby, when the children are not home or are napping, take out the toys they have not played with for a while. In a few weeks, a preschooler will forget about a lot of these toys. Every month or two, do this again by bringing out the toys that were put in storage and swap some more into storage. They will think they got a bunch of new toys and start to play with them again. If they don't play with them, then it's time to sell or donate. Sometimes, children with too many toys just get overwhelmed and won't play with any of them. They need to use their imagination more, and sometimes, they can do that better with fewer toys.

A child can clear the toy clutter at the end of each day as part of their chores. Any stray toys that are not put away properly could be collected and stored away until they are earned back over time.

The playroom should also be set up into zones and be a place for the children's imagination to take over. Within the playroom, consider themed play areas and assign specific locations for toys so the children know where each toy should be returned to at the end of playtime. Zone examples include a reading nook, art/craft area, puzzle area, dress-up/costume area, and game area. Store like items together and label containers to simplify the organization process.

If the playroom is for children of several ages, I suggest a tall bookshelf attached to the wall with an L bracket on top. That way, if you have a climber, they won't bring it all tumbling down on them. Put the cloth and board books on the bottom shelves for the toddler, and the books for older children higher out of reach so the toddler won't tear and ruin the books.

Labels for Preschoolers

Even toddlers can help pick up and put things away. Just sing the "Daniel Tiger" song while putting toys away! Since most preschoolers can't read yet, label the bins for them by using pictures of what is in the bin. You can take a photo with your phone and then move each photo to a word document. Make the photos about the size of a business card, so you can get a lot on one page. Print them out, and then if the bins are plastic, take clear tape and attach them to each bin. If you have fabric bins, you can add clear label clips to slide the photo labels into the clips. This is nice if the bins will change a lot, as it makes the labels easy to change. The child may not be able to read or spell "cars" just yet, but they know what a picture of a car or truck looks like. All the trucks and cars could be put in that bin with a photo of cars on it. That way, when you say it's time to put away your cars and trucks, they will know where they belong. This can work for dolls, train sets, play food, etc.

Entertainment Room/Home Theater

It feels great to be able to relax after a long hard day at work and watch your favorite show and sit down with a bowl of popcorn. However, when you have kids, it's hard to concentrate on the show when they are plowing through the house screaming, jumping on the furniture, or shaming you for not understanding that they want a snack right now. The space you designate as an entertainment room should be soundproof and away from everything else. Has the TV been mounted on the wall to create a seamless look?

Home theaters are becoming more popular with people who want to watch their favorite movies in the comfort of their own homes, cutting down on their travel time, and putting all their favorite movies in one place. For a small space, consider a mini projector for an entertainment center, so you can enjoy the big screen. We had some friends that were able to create a home theater in a small one bedroom apartment. They mounted the projector and pull-down screen to the ceiling. The pull-down screen was mounted on the ceiling in front of their sliding glass doors. When it was time to watch a movie they would just pull the screen down. It made the room darker which was an added bonus. When not in use the screen was rolled up and completely out of the way. Use your imagination to make your viewing area as big and comfortable as possible.

How much space do you need?

The living space has just been covered, but what about the other areas in the home? You need to have enough room to accommodate the people living there and possible guests.

Media Storage—Updating technology, for example, getting rid of VHS tapes, can save a lot of space in your home. Technology is getting smaller and more advanced with every invention, so you need to decide what you really need and where it will all go.

If you don't have the storage space, you really don't need CDs or DVDs. You can stream your music and movies online. You don't even need to have a big collection of books if you have a Kindle or other e-reader to store them on. However, there are some that will be treasured for years to come, as they have special meaning in your life, such as wedding photos or pictures of family members that you can't part with. Decide what is really necessary for you to keep and where it will all be stored.

Playrooms/areas, game rooms, and home theaters are areas that can take up lots of space and be somewhat costly. If you have enough space to separate them out, great; if not, find a way to incorporate them into your living space.

I hope these tips help you find a system that your family will enjoy using and that can make clean up time a lot easier.

Key Takeaways from This Chapter

- Use a toy bin system to separate smaller toys and keep the playroom neat.
- Create space for imagination with specific areas for arts and crafts, puzzles, dress-up, reading, and other activities.
- Purchase versatile furniture like an activity table with adjustable legs and chairs to accommodate their growth.
- Put photos on what belongs in each toy bin for quick and easy pick-up.
- Clear outdated media items that are no longer needed to save storage space in the home.

In the next chapter, we will review how to organize a home office and/or video office space.

10

HOME OFFICE AND/OR VIDEO OFFICE SPACE

"Simplicity is the ultimate sophistication."

LEONARDO DAVINCI

Do you often find yourself working from home and wondering what you should do with your space? Glad you asked! This chapter is all about how to set up a productive work environment in your own home. This section is going to be an overview of the home office. I think my next book will be about home offices and small businesses because there is just too much information to put in one chapter.

A home office just means wherever you are currently working. Work From Home (WFH) could be an office with a desk, a dining table, a kitchen counter, or even your sofa. My sofa and dining room table with my laptop is where I have my WFH office because my husband also works from home, and his office is set up in the guest bedroom. It is a good dual use for that bedroom, since most of our family is close and we don't need a guest bedroom very often. We have a daybed, his desk, file cabinet, and a couple of shelves that work well. Murphy beds (or sofa beds) work well in guest bedrooms too.

The guest bedroom/office closet is a good place to store extra office supplies. Guest bedrooms should provide a calm oasis for your guests, but its function can be multi-purposed to serve you as a home office too. The bedroom closet could also serve as your "gift wrap station." You could keep your gift wrap, bows, ribbons, enclosure cards, etc. in this closet for easy access using a hanging gift wrap station. You could also store gifts here until you are ready to wrap them. The closet can hold extra pillows, blankets, your blow-up mattress, etc.

PAPERS, PAPERS, PAPERS! These can be some of the most overwhelming. You can work days on papers and feel like you haven't done anything. Let's start with bringing in your mail. On the way back from the mailbox, start sorting the mail. Immediately put the junk mail in the trash or recycle bin. Don't even let junk mail hit your desk/table or counter. Try to handle each piece of paper once! If it is a bill, open it, throw away the outside envelope, and put the bill in the "to be paid" box. If it is something to be filed, put it in the "to be filed box."

To Be Filed

Take your "to be filed holder" and file your papers monthly into your file cabinet so it doesn't accumulate into a mountain of filing that you dread doing. Before you start filing, sort the papers into categories to view and assess each category to be sure the paper needs to be kept and filed.

If you need the paper for year-end taxes, put it in a file with all the tax documents that you will need to take to your accountant. If you do your own taxes, keep it all in one place so you won't have to go hunting for papers to start working on the taxes at year-end. If it is something that needs to be scheduled for later, put it on your calendar, for example, sending a thank you note for a gift, etc.

There are many ways to file papers. Hanging folders with the tabs all on the left is a good way to keep track of papers. Then, you can put the labeled manila file folder into the hanging file. File alphabetically according to the Pay To Name. That way, when you get the Verizon bill, you know it goes into the Verizon file folder, Frontier would be filed in the Frontier file, with the most current document at the front of the folder. Unless you use a document for a business, most papers can be thrown out after seven years. If there is personal information on the document, an office shredder is recommended.

If possible, go paperless. Set up automatic payments for monthly bills and make sure companies don't send paper mail. It is so easy now to find most documents online.

Even in a mostly paperless environment, there will still be some paper, and I want you to be able to locate any paper in under one minute!

There are only three decisions when it comes to papers: **act on it, trash it, or file it.**

Restrict items in your office space to what you really need. A pad of paper and pen are always helpful for jotting down thoughts and reminders. Noise-canceling earbuds are nice for blocking out noise and helping you focus. A calendar, either digital or paper, is a necessity when keeping your schedule in check.

Your wall outlets don't always line up in your room with where the furniture needs to be placed. An office desk usually needs several outlets. If the desk blocks the outlet, then purchase a power strip that is also a surge protector. These work wonders and they usually have 6 extra outlets and holes in the back where they can be hung on the wall or mounted to the side of a desk or shelf. You can find some that also include USB ports. If you happen to need a lamp for your desk, I suggest one like you see in hotel rooms. They include both built in USB Ports and AC Outlets! Some even have a phone stand to prop up your phone for hands free talking and offer both 2-prong and 3-prong outlets.

Separate your desk space from the storeroom. Oftentimes, we buy office products in bulk (e.g., a box of pens and a 20-pack of sticky notes). Don't keep all of them on your desk. Keep one or two of each supply at your work area but set up a separate supply space for the bulk packages. When a pen runs dry, throw it away and get another from your storage/closet area.

Let's say you just returned from vacation, and you want to keep some of those paper memories. Put those in a memorabilia box. Again, every member of the family should have a keepsake/memorabilia box with their name on it. Once a year, each family member should go through their box to see if those memories are still worth keeping. If not, throw the papers out to make room for new memories. I usually do this at the end of the year between Christmas and New Year's because the kids are home from school and have time to go through their boxes.

Helpful Apps

Todoist: A task manager that works in tandem with Gmail. There are numerous options, but my favorite is the ability to make to-do lists from actual emails, thereby eliminating the need for the email. Emails cannot be prioritized, although they may be in Todoist.

Unroll.me: Gets rid of all unwanted subscriptions. I suggest a separate email address just for subscriptions and online shopping and migrate everything to that address so your personal one is reserved exclusively for actual correspondence. Having the second Gmail address has been wonderful! I use it for all my in-person shopping and online purchases. It has worked great and kept my personal email from lots of spam.

ColorNote: This is a great place to write notes on your phone while you are on the go. It keeps reminders in one place, from short notes to longer documents.

PhotoScan: Easy and quick way to scan a lot of photos at one time. If you have old scrapbooks and don't want to take them apart for fear of destroying the photos or old paper, you can just scan them with your phone using PhotoScan and create a digital copy.

Genius Scan: A document scanner app in your pocket. Quickly scan your paper documents on the go and export them as multi-page PDF files.

Video or Zoom Rooms

Did you hear about a city mayor that decided to call a meeting dressed from the waist up but still in his underwear? When someone asked him if he was wearing pants, he wanted to know why she asked, and she said, "There is a mirror behind you!" Be sure there are no mirrors or picture frames behind you that can reflect on the video conference call. Also don't be in front of windows or open doors, as things and people going by can be distracting. Bookshelves are a great backdrop. If you don't want people to see your items, cabinets with doors can also look nice.

If you are a professional television or radio person, you can spend as much as $40,000 to remodel an office. A workspace like that can include soundproof walls, professional-grade cameras, and microphones, while also being professionally wired and attractively lit. Most of us don't need all the bells and whistles. Set up a room that has good lighting, is quiet, and does not have a lot of distractions.

Developers and home builders believe that, even after the virus is under control, the future will involve a lot more work from home, video conferencing, and remote collaboration. If you don't have time to tidy up before your next video call, you can also set up virtual backdrops on Zoom.us. If you are working from the kitchen table of a small apartment, it can be a challenge to find a private place for video conferencing. Adding a virtual background image is a good way to keep your meeting background-free and without distraction and clutter.

Key Takeaways from This Chapter

- Keep your work area simple and clutter-free so you can stay productive.
- Take advantage of those helpful apps for your home office.
- If you have the space, create a video or Zoom room.

In the next chapter, you will learn how to organize the garage, attic, and storage.

I would be very grateful if you could leave a review for *Home Clutter Cleanse* on Amazon.com!

11

GARAGE, ATTIC, AND STORAGE TIPS

"It takes as much energy to wish as it does to plan."

ELEANOR ROOSEVELT

Need more storage space? Well then, this chapter is for you!

Whether it's the outdated storage of your basement or garage, the forgotten spaces in your attic, or other unused areas around your home, there are many ways to make sure you're using every available square foot to store things.

Once your primary living areas are organized, you will feel the immediate relief of having a natural flow to your living spaces with easy access to what you need each day. The two things many households never seem to have enough of are money and storage. While I can't guarantee that going through and organizing your attic will find you lots of valuables, it is still worth the effort to clean it out and make room for the items that you need to store. Garage and attic spaces are useful storage areas. I would recommend using these spaces in the following ways, so you can easily find *what* you need and *when* you need it with the greatest ease.

Before you get started on each storage space, be sure to do S.P.A.C.E.—refer to Chapter 1 for details.

The garage becomes a short-term storage space for items you access frequently. It should be set up in "zones," so specific spaces within the garage have a purpose (tools, cars, sports, etc.). If you have several hobbies set up for example, a gardening zone, wood-working zone, etc.

Use the attic space as long-term storage. Just laying down a couple of sheets of plywood could provide some great space for this. Items stored in this space should not be needed often, so you can minimize your trips up and down the attic stairs. Things such as seasonal décor that you access only once a year, maternity clothes, clothes your child has outgrown, and archived papers could be considered for attic storage. This moves these rarely used items out of your primary living space.

If you live in a hot climate, there are many things that should not be stored in attics and garages, such as candles, old photos, leather coats, shoes, boots, and paintings. Heat and humidity can cause paint and leather to crack and expand. Your candles will take on all kinds of crazy new shapes if left in a hot garage or attic! In climates that freeze, do not store liquids in these areas because it could freeze, expand and burst open plastic containers that will begin to leak once it starts to warm up again.

Garage

Start the job again by sorting the entire contents of the garage into piles. Take everything off the shelves, off the floor, out of boxes, and out of cabinets. This will be the most time-consuming task. It is also the most important task in getting your garage organized and decluttered. Pick a nice day and use your driveway to sort, and park your car on the street or at the end of the driveway. And yes, people will ask if you are having a garage sale, so if your donation pile gets large, just tell them to make you an offer! After sorting, you will be able to see everything you own. At this point, go through each section and purge items that are no longer needed and decide whether to donate or sell.

Zones for a garage can be tools, gardening, sports, and any other hobbies you enjoy.

There are lots of overhead, ceiling-mounted storage racks that can provide great storage solutions in garages. Look for one that has a heavy load capacity. These are great for seasonal décor, luggage, and lightweight items like ice chests. They can increase your storage and clear the garage floor of clutter.

Another handy ceiling-mounted storage rack that can hold items you need to get to a little more often is a garage ceiling storage rack lift. It can help keep you off the ladder to get to your items, as you can lower the rack to the floor if needed.

I recommend at least 18" deep wire shelves with at least 5 shelves and on wheels if possible. The shelves on rolling and locking wheels are great to keep things flexible in the garage. Items stored on shelving need to be things you access more often; paint supplies, hand tools, extension cords, sporting goods, etc.

A pegboard system above a workbench for small tools keeps them within reach when you are working. You can purchase several different-sized pegs and baskets to keep your items organized.

Lowe's carries several garage bar/channel systems that attach to the studs. You can add a variety of attachments to the main track to hang yard equipment, large tools, etc. The attachments come in various shapes and sizes, and each one has a different weight capacity. The Gladiator system is my favorite brand. The Gladiator line includes cabinets with built-in doors that can often be attractive to those with OCD tendencies. Everything you need can be assigned a shelf with like items in the cabinet, but the door closes, and you don't have to "see" the inventory you own. They have gear track channels that are great for hanging different-sized items on the wall such as shovels, rakes, brooms, and other yard equipment.

Storage containers should not be any larger than 18-gallon clear storage totes. Any larger and when full will get too heavy to lift.

Cardboard boxes tend to attract insects, so I recommend you use plastic tubs for storing items in the garage. I especially like the clear weathertight totes with latched lids for garages to guard against the elements and insects. Just add a label to each tote so you can easily find what you need when you need it. The Container Store also carries a line of well-made garage totes.

Since cardboard boxes should not be used for long time storage, use your leftover boxes for sorting and donations as you begin the organizing process.

Sport Zone

Sports Net Bags—These can be hung on a hook in the garage to hold tennis balls, baseballs, pool toys, etc.

A laundry basket is great for holding balls for younger children. They can easily reach them and put them away when cleaning up.

A rolling laundry sorter is great for holding equipment separated by sport or child. The bins are deep enough to hold bats, hockey sticks, skateboards, and helmets.

Many children are in different sports and usually have to take items with them to practice or games. I suggest a mesh bag to hold their items, like water bottles, baseball gloves, etc. Add a luggage tag with their name and list the items needed for the activity so you can check the list quickly before leaving the house. Hang these bags close to the door so they can be easily grabbed as you and your family run out the door to the next practice event.

An umbrella stand can be repurposed to hold bats, golf clubs, and hockey sticks. A pegboard with hooks can hold bike helmets, gear bags, and skateboards.

Vertical wall space is great to hang fishing rods, snow skis, surf boards, etc. Wire baskets make a nice holder for roller skates or ice skates.

Vehicles

A bin to organize items such as coupons, reusable grocery bags, and things you wish to return to the store will be particularly useful to have in your car. A collapsible (large cloth according type) trunk-organizing bin is very useful.

Purchase a trash can for your vehicle. For your store and restaurant coupons-get a clear plastic zip-lock bag to place between your seat and the console of your car. Many times, when my husband and I can't decide where we would like to eat, I just grab the bag to see what restaurant coupons we can use. Clean this out often because they do expire (we have found that some of our favorite restaurants will take expired coupons, so it doesn't hurt to ask!)

This is a list of handy items to keep in your car - Phone chargers, First Aid Kit, flashlight, pen and paper, seatbelt cutter and window breaker, sunscreen, tissues and cash/change for toll roads. If you have small children, also carry a bag with wet wipes, diapers, and a change of clothes. A backseat organizer that attaches to the back of the seat is a great place for their toys and books.

Vehicle Apps

Where's My Car: Locates your parked car

Waze: Traffic and GPS navigation similar to Google Maps

Pets

Our pets are like members of our family. Like any member of the family, there are tips for organizing their things too. Pets can cause all manner of chaos, so it is best to plan ahead. Start by creating a simple schedule for feeding, playtime, walks, etc.

Taking care of a beloved family pet is a full-time job. It may seem overwhelming, but it will be easier if you have the right supplies on hand. Organizing the supplies you need is a good place to start.

1. Pet Food Storage

Pet food can be an organization challenge. Store pet food in a rolling container with an airtight seal so you can contain the food smell. Food smells can attract pests and spoil your other goods. Find an airtight container that fits your needs. The containers should have translucent sides so you can easily see when it is time to buy more food.

2. Keep the Feeding Area Clean

Pet food spills are a mess. Keep the feeding area clean by placing an absorbent mat under the food and water bowls. A spill-containing pet dish set is a good idea on top of the absorbent mat. The splash guard rim collects water or kibble, so spills will not cause a slipping hazard. It also protects floors and walls from stains, mold, and damage. Neater Pets Feeders also come in different colors and sizes, which makes it easy for you to find the one that fits your home.

3. Pet Supply Organizer

Pet supplies can also be a cluttered mess. Gather all the supplies in one area to save yourself from excess trips. Keep your space organized with an all-in-one pet organizer. This product is mounted on the wall in the hall near the door to hang leashes, stash training treats, and more. This convenient home for dog-walking essentials means you can always find them when you are ready to go. It is a great tool for pet owners who need to organize their pet supplies. It is compact, lightweight, and easy to place anywhere.

Some pets like outside toys. Store the toys in a plastic laundry basket. It makes it easy to wash the toys and the rain water runs out of the laundry basket.

Pet odors can be hard to recognize by the owner living around the pet full time. We can truly become "nose blind!" Clean litter boxes daily and wash the pet beds regularly. When your pet has an accident, use an enzyme cleaner promptly to break down the smell. Ask a family member that does not live in your home to do a smell test and to let you know when there is an odor issue!

Fun Tip—Wall space is oftentimes forgotten in garages, closets, and attics. A great way to store large wreaths is in large, clear, heavy-duty plastic trash bags. It keeps the dust off; you can see what is in the bag, and is easy to hang on the wall. They make smaller clear bags too that can be used to store out-of-season clothes in your closets. The large clear bags are great for storing baby toys and equipment that are waiting for the next baby. The bags are nice for storing items in the garage because things in there can get dusty quickly.

Key Takeaways from This Chapter

- Garages are great for storage; organize your garage in zones to be functional, and efficient!
- Your attic is a perfect place for long term storage; organized properly, it is an amazing space saver for rarely used items.
- Organize and store items in your car so you are prepared for the unexpected while traveling.
- Pets are a huge part of our households; they need organized storage areas as well.

CLUTTER, CLUTTER, CLUTTER

"Bottom line is, if you do not use it or need it, it's cluttered, and it needs to go."

CHARISSE WARD

Clutter comes in the form of many different things. These can be keepsakes, papers/mail/magazines, books, collectibles, photos, crafts, sports items, cookbooks, clothes, shoes, purses, hats, etc.

As many others have said, if it doesn't serve a purpose, get rid of it.

If you have too much stuff to fit into, for example, a linen closet, then you need to make a choice as to what to keep and what not to keep. Old towels can be ripped in two and used as rags in the garage, old sheets can become drop cloths for painting or covering outdoor furniture to keep the dust off.

It is easier to remove clutter than it is to create storage space. I met an older couple that wanted to move closer to their children and downsize at the same time. They had an estate sale, and the husband did a great job of pricing his items and sold most of what he had in the garage. The wife, on the other hand, had owned an antique store and felt that all the old collectibles were worth much more than they really were, and most of the items in the house did not sell. I later found out they had five more storage units full of her items. When your stuff starts costing more than it's worth, it's time to really purge! Storage units should only be temporary. Again, if you have had a unit for more than a year, then it's time to purge, especially if you haven't gotten anything from it and probably haven't missed it. Sell or donate ASAP and put that money toward something you enjoy!

I don't believe, like some organizers do, that you have to get rid of everything and live like a minimalist. If you like that idea, great, but it is not a requirement to get your items organized and life decluttered.

Ownership can often be overrated. We believe we need to own something to enjoy it, and that's not true. We may get more pleasure out of borrowing or renting an item. Everything we own requires that we clean, store, move, repair, and maybe even pay extra to insure it! This all takes time and energy. Think out of the box on alternative ways to access and enjoy physical objects. Our family is fortunate enough to all live within a half-hour of each other. Both our son and son-in-law are do-it-yourselfers when it comes to their homes and cars. My husband and I are also DIYers. Instead of all three of us having to store large tools, we share some, for example, a portable table saw that our son owns and stores in his garage. We own and store the large compressor. If you don't have family close, possibly find friends that have the same interests and are willing to share or perhaps create a co-op of sharing.

I'm not a fan of cooking but would love to organize your kitchen after you make me a meal! I love helping people! If you don't want to do this yourself, find friends or family members to help and keep you on task. In turn, do something for them that you like to do! Cooking, running errands for them, etc.

Once you have decluttered your home and gotten organized, here are a few websites that can help you with storage planning or redecorating-

Planning Storage—IKEA's Planning Tools

https://www.ikea.com/us/en/planners/

Planning Storage—The Container Store's Design Planner

https://www.containerstore.com/design-center

Designing and furniture layouts—Homestyler

https://www.homestyler.com/

Designing a kitchen—Lowe's Virtual Room Designer

https://www.lowes.com/l/about/virtual-room-designer

Paint colors—PPG Paints' Paint Color Visualizer

https://www.ppgpaints.com/color/color-tools/visualizer

Designing landscaping or patio—Better Homes & Gardens Plan-A-Garden

https://www.bhg.com/gardening/design/nature-lovers/welcome-to-plan-a-garden/

Calculate how much material (tile, mulch, etc.) to buy for a project—Home Depot's Project Calculators

https://www.homedepot.com/c/project_calculators

When should I hire a Professional Organizer?

If this all seems too overwhelming, or you are not physically able to do the work, then you might want to consider hiring a Professional Organizer, and here are the reasons why.

We work with many people recovering from an accident, have had health issues, and don't have the strength to do the work needed. Many times, if we can just get the home organized for them, they can maintain the systems. If not, we also have clients that we visit once a week or monthly to help them maintain an organized home.

Again, Professional Organizers often help people going through major life changes. Times of upheaval and stress such as divorce, moving into a new home, death in the family, or possibly a new baby in the family can all be major stressors. We try to empathize with the client, knowing that grappling with feelings of grief or anxiety are present during major changes. If we can take care of that empty bedroom once the child has left for college or get the nursery organized, they can sort through their emotions and adjust to life changes once the task is completed.

Organizers have various specialties, such as emergency preparedness, genealogy research, digital clutter, collections, and memorabilia. Some organizers get extra training to help clients who suffer from physical disabilities, senior downsizing, ADHD, OCD, or hoarding. Organizers help people manage their tasks, encourage their clients to avoid procrastination, and help them with time management.

Remember that Professional Organizers are not judging you! So many times, when we enter a new client's home or business, they start apologizing. "This must be the worst place you have ever seen! I'm so embarrassed!" We have seen a lot, and to us, it's exciting because we are there to help.

One of our ongoing clients is hooked on QVC and other shopping networks. He is a retired gentleman that lives alone. The sad thing is that I think he is just bored and lonely and has the money to buy things that he may never use. The first time we walked into his house, the entire living room was full of unopened Amazon/shipping boxes. It took us days just to get everything opened and sorted. Whenever he couldn't find something in his house, he would just order it again. For example, we found, unopened, 12 sets of fingernail clippers. When asked if he wanted to keep a couple and donate the rest, the response was that they were hard to find, and he needed to keep all 12 sets! Funny he was able to find 12 of them! That is why the purge process may take longer with some people. He did have lots of other duplicates that he donated. Many were brand new, never opened.

Professional Organizers are not trying to make you get rid of everything! Although some people like extreme minimalism and limit themselves to only 100 items, most organizers care more about how your stuff works for you and your lifestyle and couldn't care less about how many items you own. You only need to get rid of things when you don't have the space to keep them or no longer use them. We want you to have a level of stuff that is right for you, so you won't be overwhelmed.

Hoarders

There are semi hoarders, and then there are the gross ones you have seen on TV. The gross hoarders are charged at a higher rate and can even require special equipment. Think hazmat suit, (just kidding...almost!). Hoarders can take a lot of time because you first need them to trust you and recognize that you are there to help. They also need to think through things more, so it doesn't happen again.

Since we are moving into a more mobile society, people don't collect as much as they used to. As you see in other books, minimalism is trending. If you think your collection of Elvis CDs is ever going to be worth something, please check the demand on eBay. Nowadays, you can hardly give away that beautifully flowered 12-piece set of Noritake China. I know it was your loved one's, but if you are not using it, sell it on eBay because it is taking up space you could use for other things. Check first if your children or other family members want an item. If not, take a photo and donate it so someone else can enjoy it. That way, you will have more room for the things you do use and enjoy.

As you age, you realize things are not as important as people and those you love. If your "things" are standing in the way of having guests come to your house or causing problems in your life, then they need to go. One client had filled up his 1-bedroom apartment with boxes and boxes of books, CDs, and DVDs. He had over 30 56-quart plastic trunk containers full of DVDs, CDs, VHS, album, cassettes, misc. papers, books, magazines, photos, and keepsakes. There were Beatles CDs, Elvis DVDs, Little Mermaid Cards and collectibles, etc. Every space along the walls of the apartment was stacked to the ceiling with containers. It was really sad because this was the second time in fewer than three years that he had an organizer in to help him with the clutter. His sister paid for us to do the job, but he wouldn't get rid of hardly anything. He had a girlfriend that he wanted to marry. The girlfriend told him that if he didn't clean up the mess, that was not going to happen. We encouraged him to find the value of his collections and start selling if there was a market. We did the best we could, but we're not sure if he ever got married.

One of my favorite sayings from Larry Burket, financial planner was "Do your giving while you're living so you knowing where it's going." Since we now have grown children with families of their own, I have started giving them keepsakes from their childhood or items that were their grandparents', etc. Some things they really appreciated when they started having kids included a wooden rocking horse that was handmade for my son that I had kept on a high shelf in the garage all these years. We had lots of photos of him on it, so now he can take photos of his children on the rocking horse. We downsized several years ago, so I don't have the storage space I used to have. I too have to confess that I also kept silly keepsakes, but after a while, I just couldn't throw them away. The funniest one was our children's baby teeth. I finally gave the small boxes of teeth to them and told them they could throw them away, but I just couldn't do it. Our daughter-in-law, who is not sentimental at all, immediately threw her husband's teeth in the trash! We all need to learn to let it go! That is when I realized that if they don't want these keepsakes, why am I holding on to them? You need to ask yourself the same question with many of your items. Does anyone in the family want these keepsakes? If not, do your family a favor and start getting rid of stuff today so they won't have to deal with it when you are gone. If you aren't using it, it doesn't fit, is out of style, you don't like it anymore, no one else wants it, DONATE, SELL, OR TRASH! I hate seeing landfills creating sky-high mountains of trash, so if you think anyone else can use your items, please donate! Many times, people break the lid of their favorite casserole dish, so even if you only have the lid, donate it because it will be a great find for someone else that needs it!

Purging never ends. Commit to purging continually. It is easier if you do this daily rather than once a year. Keep those donation boxes handy in closets and your garage! Decluttering is needed through different seasons of our lives, such as with a growing family, retirement, merging homes in a marriage, etc.

Before an item enters your home, ask yourself, do I have space for this? Do I really need this? What am I willing to get rid of so I can have room for the new item?

I have a yard sale every year, sometimes twice a year. It is an enjoyable activity and fun to meet the buyers of my stuff! It gives me a deadline to work toward and a motivation to let go because I can also make money! After the sale, we pack up most of what is left and take it to a donation drop-off site. Every time after the sale, I think I have gotten rid of everything, but somehow, my yard sale closet starts to fill up again, and I am in need of another sale. I usually make at least $100 (sometimes as much as $600 if I am selling furniture, etc.), and most items are priced at $1.00, so you know I am getting rid of a lot of stuff. That is why it is so important when going through a drawer, closet, changing seasons, taking down decorations, etc. to put unused or unwanted items in a designated area like a yard sale closet. The purging never stops. It helps me know that when I am buying something new, I can repay myself by selling an old item. It's like getting a deal on the upgrade (or that's how I justify the new item to my husband!).

Good Professional Organizers can help you save money. They have insider knowledge and relationships with many different vendors, such as moving companies, junk pickup, closet shelving, and vetted handymen. They can recommend good estate sale companies or antique experts.

When we were working with a client organizing the files in his office, we found cash and gift cards totaling over $3,000 (some of the mail hadn't even been opened). We had one client with a vehicle they wanted to sell but couldn't find the title. While cleaning out the garage, we found the title. We found a 1 ½ carat diamond ring for another client. We have found wills, other jewelry, lost Amazon Kindles, tools, antiques, and keepsakes, all of which have made our clients very happy!

Pros and Cons of Hiring a Professional Organizer (PO)

If you do hire a PO, here are some suggestions. If they are organizing your kitchen or bedroom closets, get caught up on dirty dishes and laundry. POs are not maids or housekeepers. We will take the clean dishes out of the dishwasher to put them in the correct cabinet, but if you have a counter full of dirty dishes, we are not going to wash them or load the dishwasher. We will wipe out or sweep the areas when we are putting things away, but that is about as far as it goes for cleaning (besides cleaning up after ourselves after organizing). Same with dirty clothes. We will put the dirty clothes all in one pile close to the washing machine, but most Professional Organizers will not do the laundry. If you have a pile of clean clothes on the bed and have enough hangers, we will hang them up for you and put them in the closet or drawers, depending on the item. If most of the washing is done prior to our arrival, we will know how to organize your place better because we will be able to see everything you own for each closet, cabinet, etc.

Go around the entire home with a trash bag and pick up all the trash like old magazines, papers, etc. so we know that what is left are things you want to keep. Our clients are always very involved in the purging process! Unless you tell us to throw something away, it will probably get sorted, and you will need to look at it and let us know if you want to keep the item or not. If we are sorting trash, the process will just take longer and cost you more money.

DIY	Hire a PO
Free	Cost
Overwhelmed, not physically able or too tired to start	Many hands make light work
Can take a lot of time for each room	Because of their experience, they can quickly make a plan for each room. That normally means moving furniture, buying containers, shelves, etc.

REFERENCES

Allen, T. (n.d.). "To me, the kitchen is a place of adventure and entirely fun, not drudgery. I can't think of anything better to do with family and friends than to be together to create something." *BrainyQuote.* Retrieved from https://www.brainyquote.com/quotes/ted_allen_443536

Aubrey, Allison. (2016). A Cluttered Kitchen Can Nudge Us to Overeat. Retrieved on 04/01/2021 from: https://www.npr.org/sections/the-salt/2016/02/15/466567647/a-cluttered-kitchen-can-nudge-us-to-overeat-study-finds

Buchwald, A. (n.d.) "Dinner is not what you do in the evening before something else. Dinner is the evening." *GoodReads.* Retrieved from https://www.goodreads.com/quotes/666519-dinner-is-not-what-you-do-in-the-evening-before

Conran, T. (n.d.). "The living room should be a place where we feel totally at ease." *AZQuotes.* Retrieved from https://www.azquotes.com/quote/866016

da Vinci, L. (n.d.). "Simplicity is the ultimate sophistication." *GoodReads*. Retrieved from https://www.goodreads.com/quotes/9010638-simplicity-is-the-ultimate-sophistication-when-once-you-have-tasted

Daniel Tiger's Neighborhood. (2015). *Daniel Tiger theme song* [Video]. YouTube. https://www.youtube.com/watch?v=IDaDSDPWvbw.

Dutton, Judy. (2012). Make Your Bed, Change Your Life. Retrieved on 04/01/2021 from: https://www.psychologytoday.com/us/blog/brain-candy/201208/make-your-bed-change-your-life

Franklin, B. (n.d.). "A place for everything, everything in its place." *Brainy-Quote*. Retrieved from https://www.brainyquote.com/quotes/benjamin_franklin_109062

Haas, Susan Biali M.D. (2011). What your Clutter Big or Small is Trying to Tell you. Retrieved on 03/17/2021 from: https://www.psychologytoday.com/us/blog/prescriptions-life/201101/what-your-clutter-big-or-small-is-trying-tell-you

Krauss Whitbourne, Susan, Ph.D. (2017). 5 Reasons Why Clutter Disrupts Mental Health Retrieved on 03/13/2021. From: https://www.psychologytoday.com/us/blog/fulfillment-any-age/201705/5-reasons-why-clutter-disrupts-mental-health

Roosevelt, E. (n.d.). "It takes as much energy to wish as it does to plan." *BrainyQuote*. Retrieved from https://www.brainyquote.com/quotes/eleanor_roosevelt_379411

Ryback, Ralph, M.D. (2016). The Powerful Psychology Behind Cleanliness. Retrieved on 04/05/2021 from: https://www.psychologytoday.-com/us/blog/the-truisms-wellness/201607/the-powerful-psychology-behind-cleanliness

Sanders, Libby, (2019). What does Clutter do to Your Brain and Body Retrieved on 03/16/2021 from: https://www1.racgp.org.au/newsgp/clinical/what-does-clutter-do-to-your-brain-and-body.

Sapna. (2017). Motivational Monday: For every minute spent organizing, an hour is earned. *The Teaching Cove*. Retrieved from https://www.teachingcove.com/motivate/every-minute-spent-organizing/

Schofield, D. (1994). "Work at getting organized is like a hobby. Set aside a certain amount of time each day (or whatever time your budget will allow). While it may indeed take a fair amount of time to establish order, once it is achieved, you will save more time than you have ever spent." From *Confessions of an organized homemaker: the secrets of uncluttering your home and taking control of your life*. Retrieved from https://www.azquotes.com/author/82121-Deniece_Schofield

Scott, J. (n.d.). "The sole purpose of the bedroom is to melt away any stressors." · *BrainyQuote*. Retrieved from https://www.brainyquote.com/quotes/jonathan_scott_1004574

Staff at Promises Behavior Health. (2020). Clutter Addiction. Retrieved on 03/15/2021 from: https://www.promisesbehavioralhealth.com/addiction-recovery-blog/clutter-addiction/

Swindoll, C. R. (n.d.). "Each day of our lives we make deposits in the memory banks of our children. *BrainyQuote*. Retrieved from https://www.brainyquote.com/quotes/charles_r_swindoll_106981

Ward, C. (n.d.). "Bottom line is, if you do not use it or need it, it's clutter, and it needs to go." *Quotetab*. Retrieved from https://www.quotetab.com/quote/by-charisse-ward/bottom-line-is-if-you-do-not-use-it-or-need-it-its-clutter-and-it-needs-to-go

Wedge, Marilyn. Ph.D. (2016). Clutter is a Relationship Issue. Retrieved on 03/16/2021 from: https://www.psychologytoday.com/us/blog/suffer-the-children/201607/cluttering-is-relationship-issue

Printed in Great Britain
by Amazon

77593132R00078